TOP 10: THE FORTY-NINERS

A PREQUEL TO TOP 10

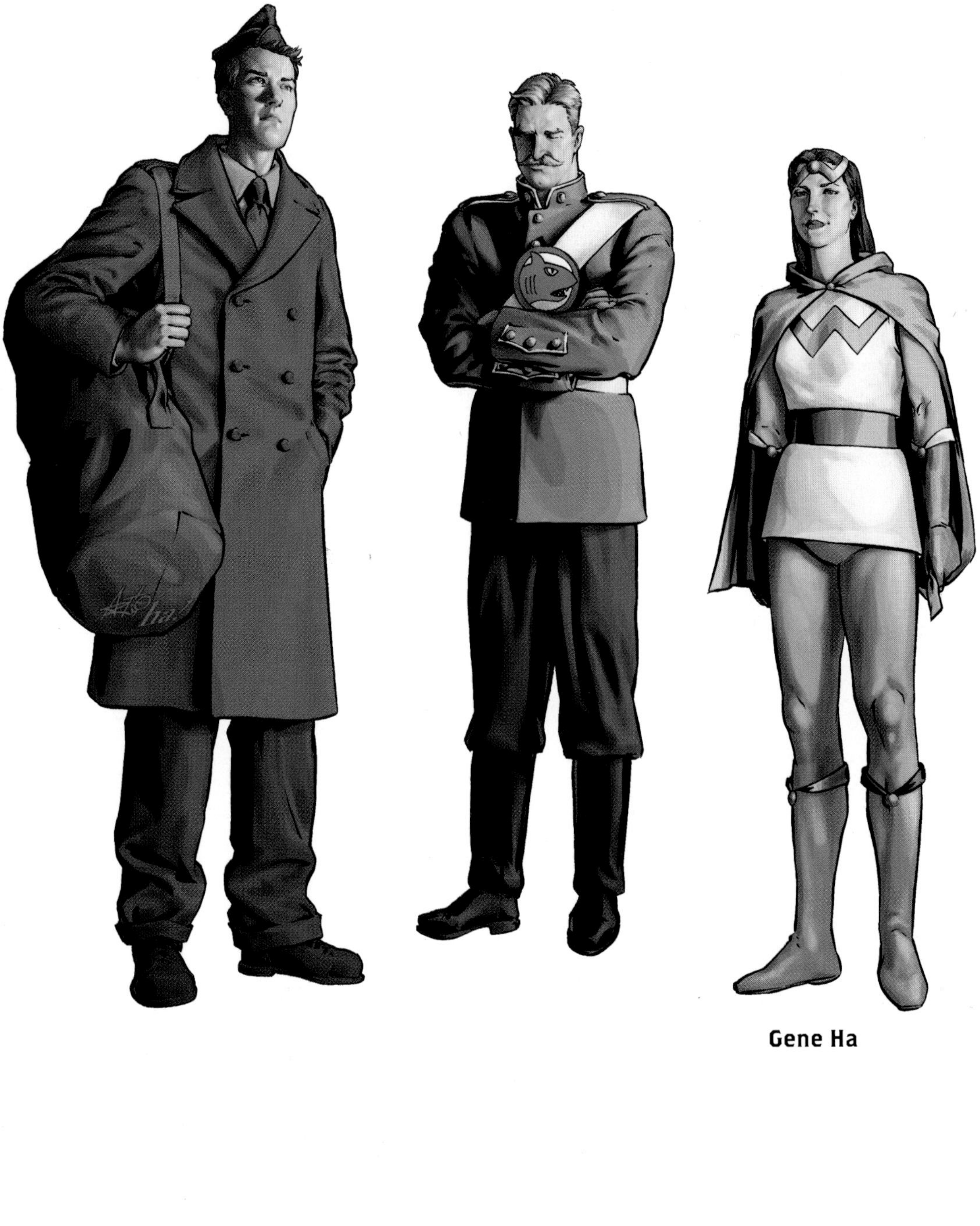

Gene Ha

JIM LEE
Editorial Director

JOHN NEE
VP – Business Development

SCOTT DUNBIER
Executive Editor

KRISTY QUINN
Assistant Editor

TOP 10 THE FORTY-NINERS

ALAN MOORE
writer

GENE HA
artist

ART LYON
colorist

TODD KLEIN
lettering, logos
and design

created by Alan Moore and Gene Ha

AMERICA'S
BEST COMICS

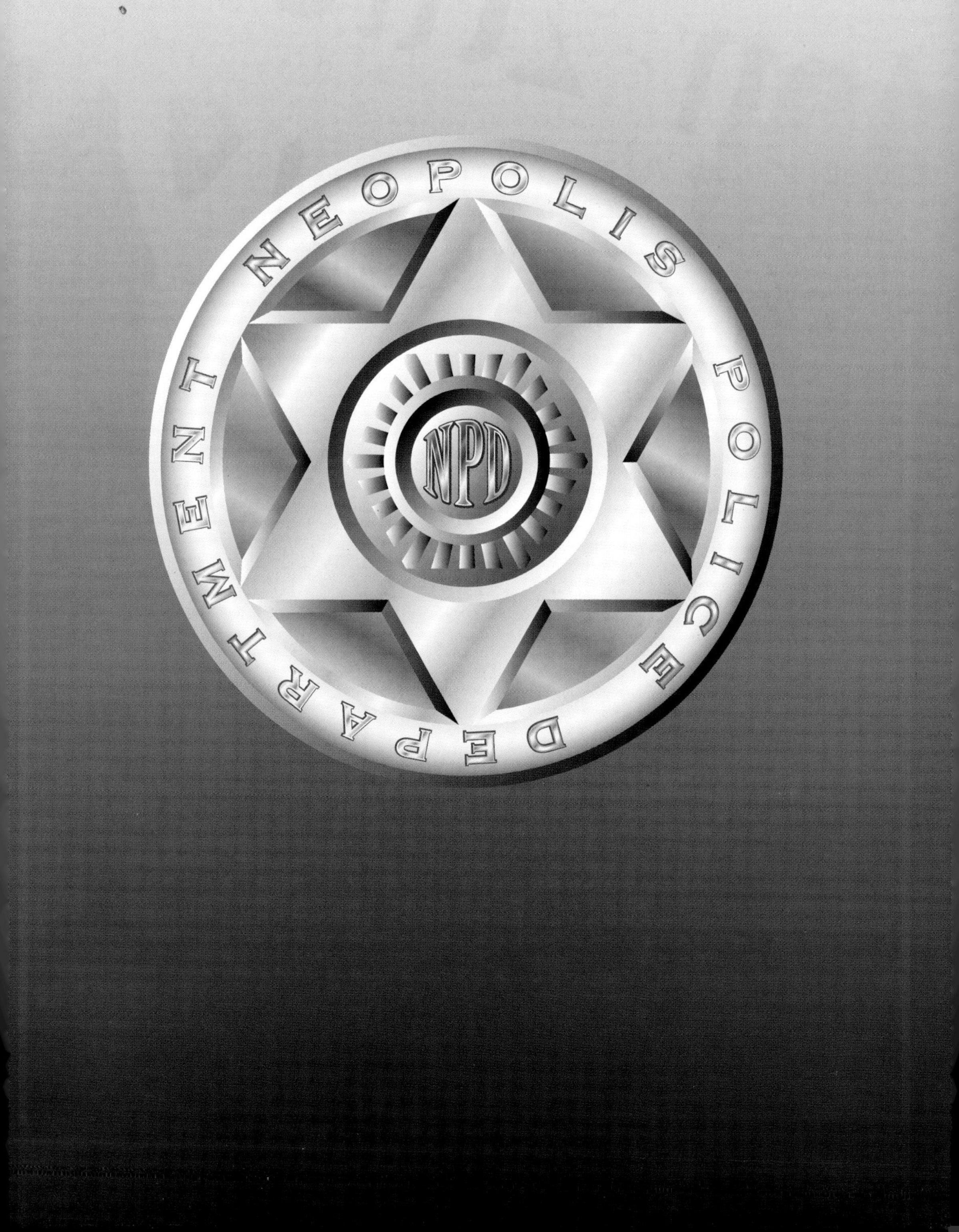
NEOPOLIS POLICE DEPARTMENT
NPD

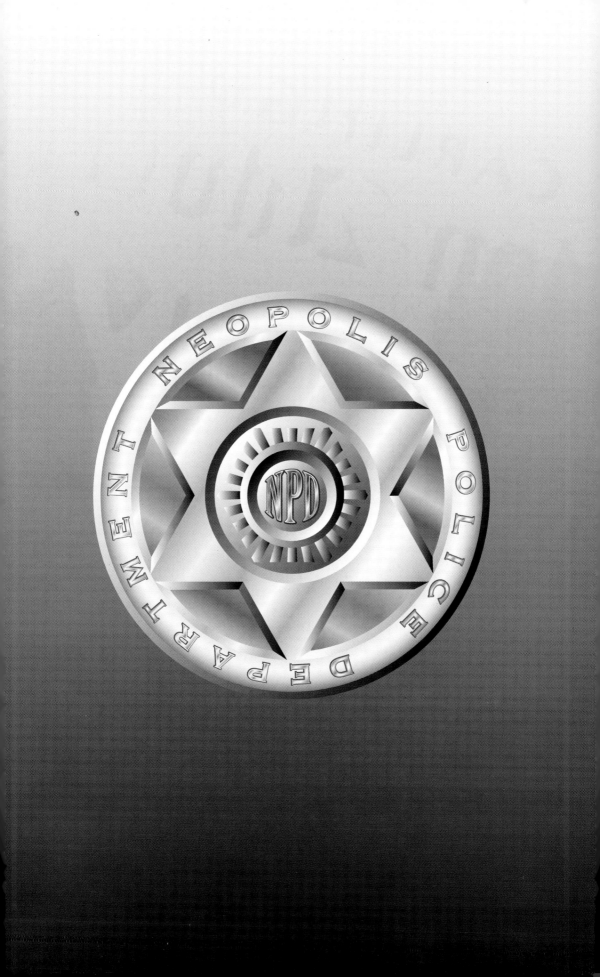

CARLINGDALE

Clarion-Advertiser

5¢ DAILY

MONDAY, AUGUST 1st, 1949

NEW ARRIVALS EXPECTED TO...

...or Genovese ...ddress crowd ...ity Hall

...EOPOLIS EXCLUSIVE BY
...MANNY DEGREGORIO

...Johnny Genovese has wasted no time in
... the city's new government registration
...location plan into operation, with his office
...overseeing the paperwork mandated by the
...dent's advisors and working together with
...h the State Department and the War Veterans'
...ministration, the Mayor was upbeat about the

Government ... boost city ec... population

Economists weigh...

While longtime residents of the...
anxious about the massive chan...
L. Wobble of the Economics...
burg says that the future hold...
"We can't continue to t...
brought us to a juncture th...

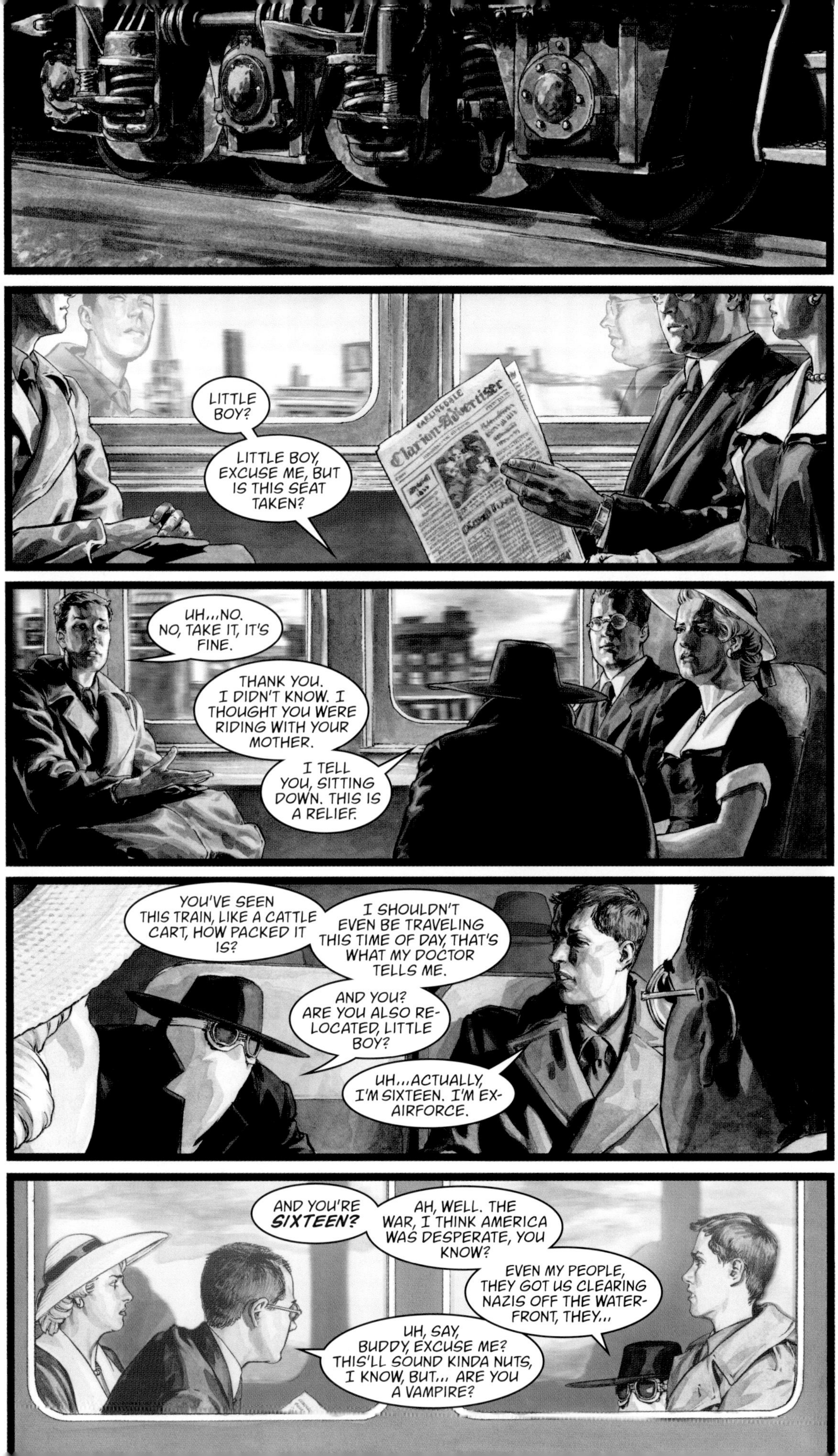

LITTLE BOY?
LITTLE BOY, EXCUSE ME, BUT IS THIS SEAT TAKEN?
UH...NO. NO, TAKE IT, IT'S FINE.
THANK YOU. I DIDN'T KNOW. I THOUGHT YOU WERE RIDING WITH YOUR MOTHER.
I TELL YOU, SITTING DOWN. THIS IS A RELIEF.
YOU'VE SEEN THIS TRAIN, LIKE A CATTLE CART, HOW PACKED IT IS?
I SHOULDN'T EVEN BE TRAVELING THIS TIME OF DAY, THAT'S WHAT MY DOCTOR TELLS ME.
AND YOU? ARE YOU ALSO RE-LOCATED, LITTLE BOY?
UH...ACTUALLY, I'M SIXTEEN. I'M EX-AIRFORCE.
AND YOU'RE SIXTEEN?
AH, WELL. THE WAR, I THINK AMERICA WAS DESPERATE, YOU KNOW?
EVEN MY PEOPLE, THEY GOT US CLEARING NAZIS OFF THE WATER-FRONT, THEY...
UH, SAY, BUDDY, EXCUSE ME? THIS'LL SOUND KINDA NUTS, I KNOW, BUT... ARE YOU A VAMPIRE?

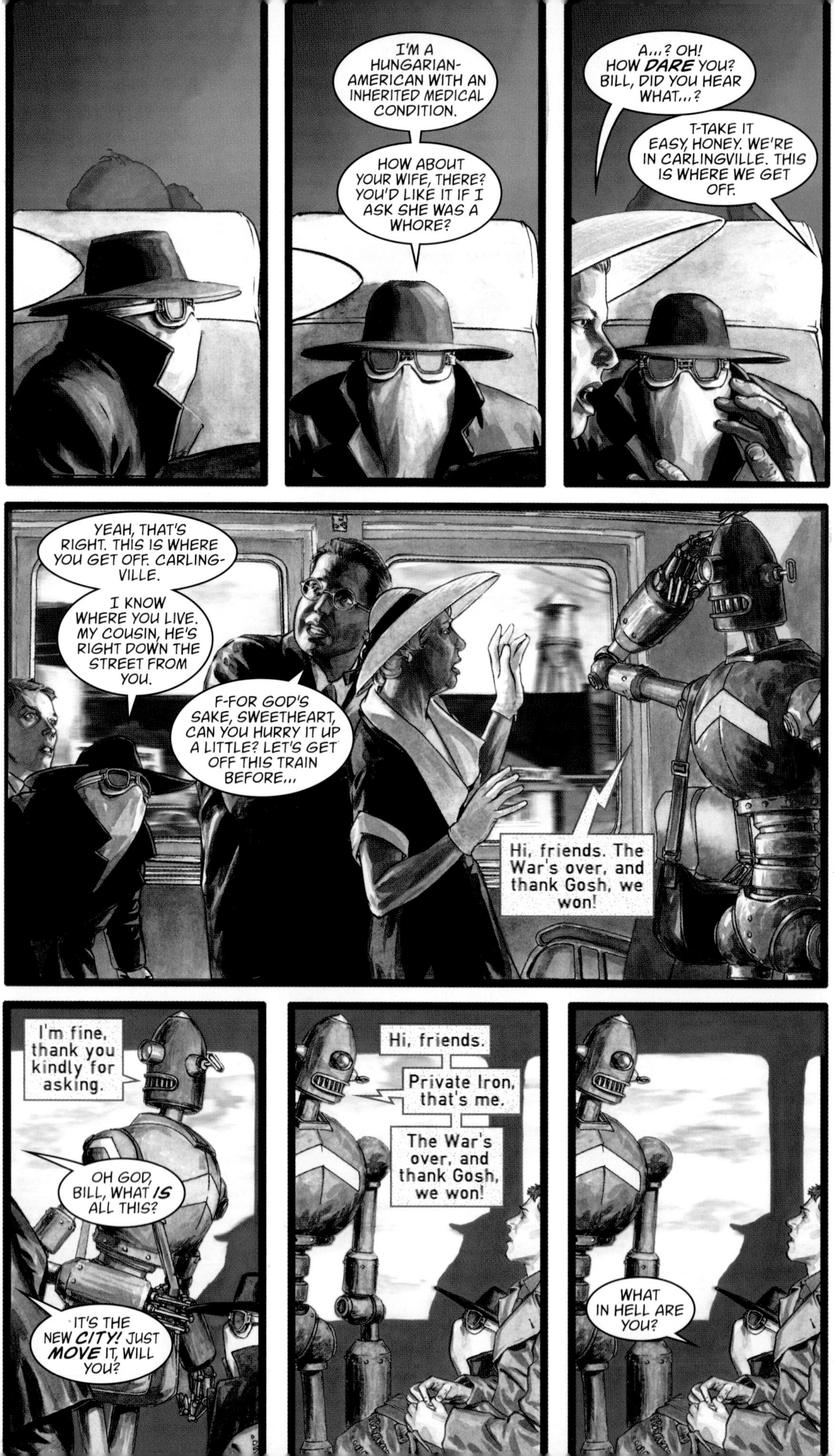
I'M A HUNGARIAN-AMERICAN WITH AN INHERITED MEDICAL CONDITION.
HOW ABOUT YOUR WIFE, THERE? YOU'D LIKE IT IF I ASK SHE WAS A WHORE?
A...? OH! HOW DARE YOU? BILL, DID YOU HEAR WHAT...?
T-TAKE IT EASY, HONEY. WE'RE IN CARLINGVILLE. THIS IS WHERE WE GET OFF.
YEAH, THAT'S RIGHT. THIS IS WHERE YOU GET OFF. CARLING-VILLE.
I KNOW WHERE YOU LIVE. MY COUSIN, HE'S RIGHT DOWN THE STREET FROM YOU.
F-FOR GOD'S SAKE, SWEETHEART, CAN YOU HURRY IT UP A LITTLE? LET'S GET OFF THIS TRAIN BEFORE...
Hi, friends. The War's over, and thank Gosh, we won!
I'm fine, thank you kindly for asking.
OH GOD, BILL, WHAT IS ALL THIS?
IT'S THE NEW CITY! JUST MOVE IT, WILL YOU?
Hi, friends.
Private Iron, that's me.
The War's over, and thank Gosh, we won!
WHAT IN HELL ARE YOU?

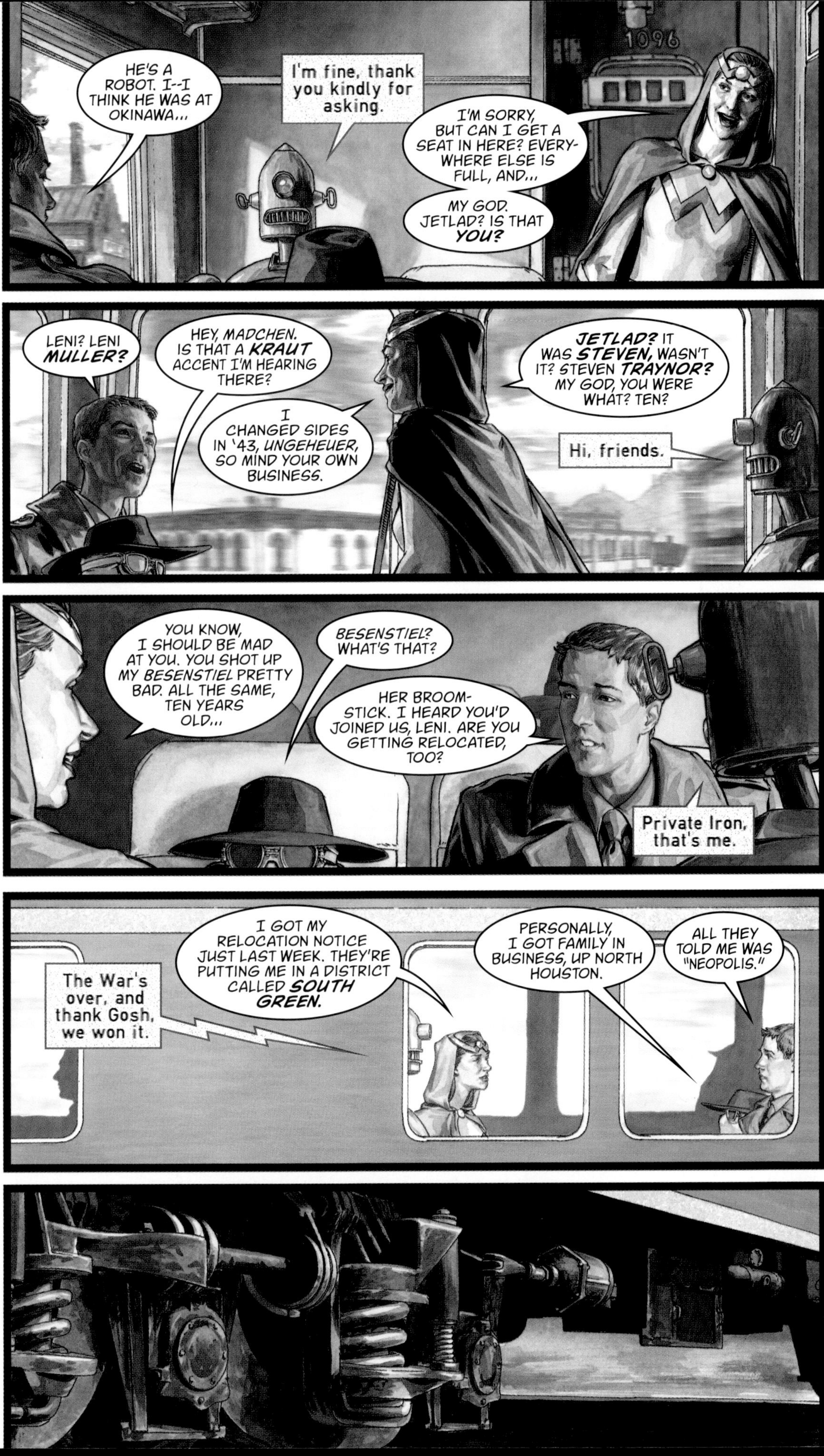
1096
HE'S A ROBOT. I--I THINK HE WAS AT OKINAWA...
I'm fine, thank you kindly for asking.
I'M SORRY, BUT CAN I GET A SEAT IN HERE? EVERY-WHERE ELSE IS FULL, AND...
MY GOD. JETLAD? IS THAT *YOU?*
LENI? LENI *MULLER?*
HEY, *MADCHEN.* IS THAT A *KRAUT* ACCENT I'M HEARING THERE?
I CHANGED SIDES IN '43, *UNGEHEUER,* SO MIND YOUR OWN BUSINESS.
JETLAD? IT WAS *STEVEN,* WASN'T IT? STEVEN *TRAYNOR?* MY GOD, YOU WERE WHAT? TEN?
Hi, friends.
YOU KNOW, I SHOULD BE MAD AT YOU. YOU SHOT UP MY *BESENSTIEL* PRETTY BAD. ALL THE SAME, TEN YEARS OLD...
BESENSTIEL? WHAT'S THAT?
HER BROOM-STICK. I HEARD YOU'D JOINED US, LENI. ARE YOU GETTING RELOCATED, TOO?
Private Iron, that's me.
The War's over, and thank Gosh, we won it.
I GOT MY RELOCATION NOTICE JUST LAST WEEK. THEY'RE PUTTING ME IN A DISTRICT CALLED *SOUTH GREEN.*
PERSONALLY, I GOT FAMILY IN BUSINESS, UP NORTH HOUSTON.
ALL THEY TOLD ME WAS "NEOPOLIS."

FORTY-NINERS

CHAPTER 1
WHAT IS BELIEVABLE AFTER WAR

FRAMING at
116 FULTON ST
STARR
FRAME PICTURE Co

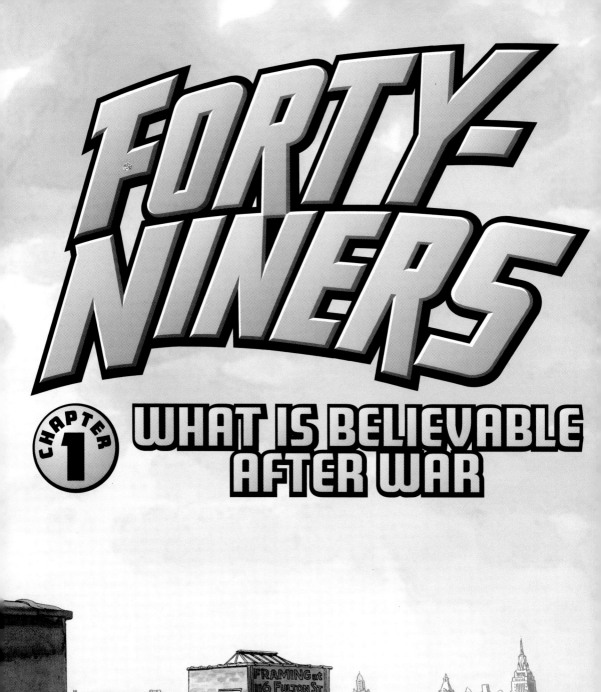

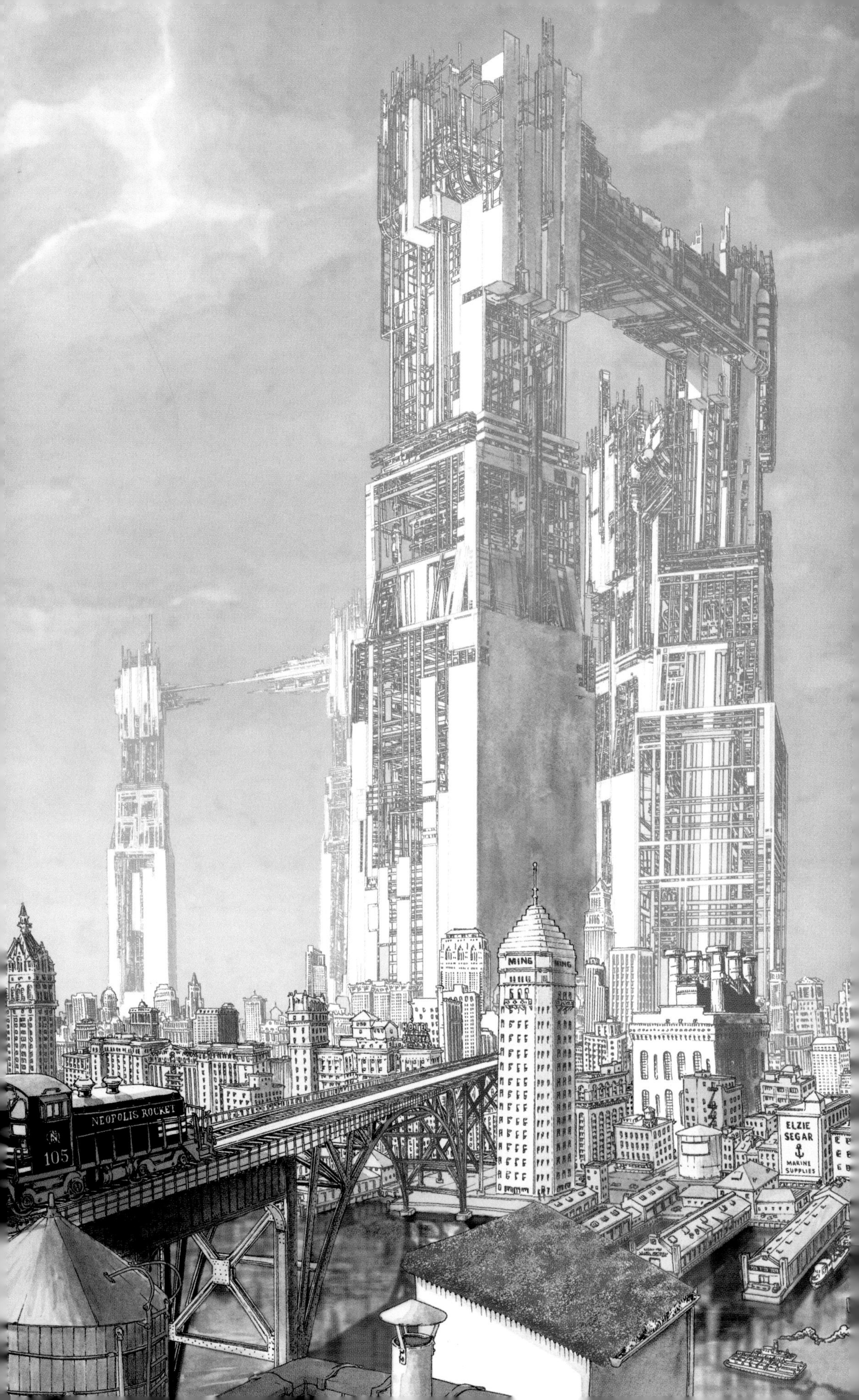
NEOPOLIS ROCKET
105
MING
MING
ELZIE SEGAR
MARINE SUPPLIES

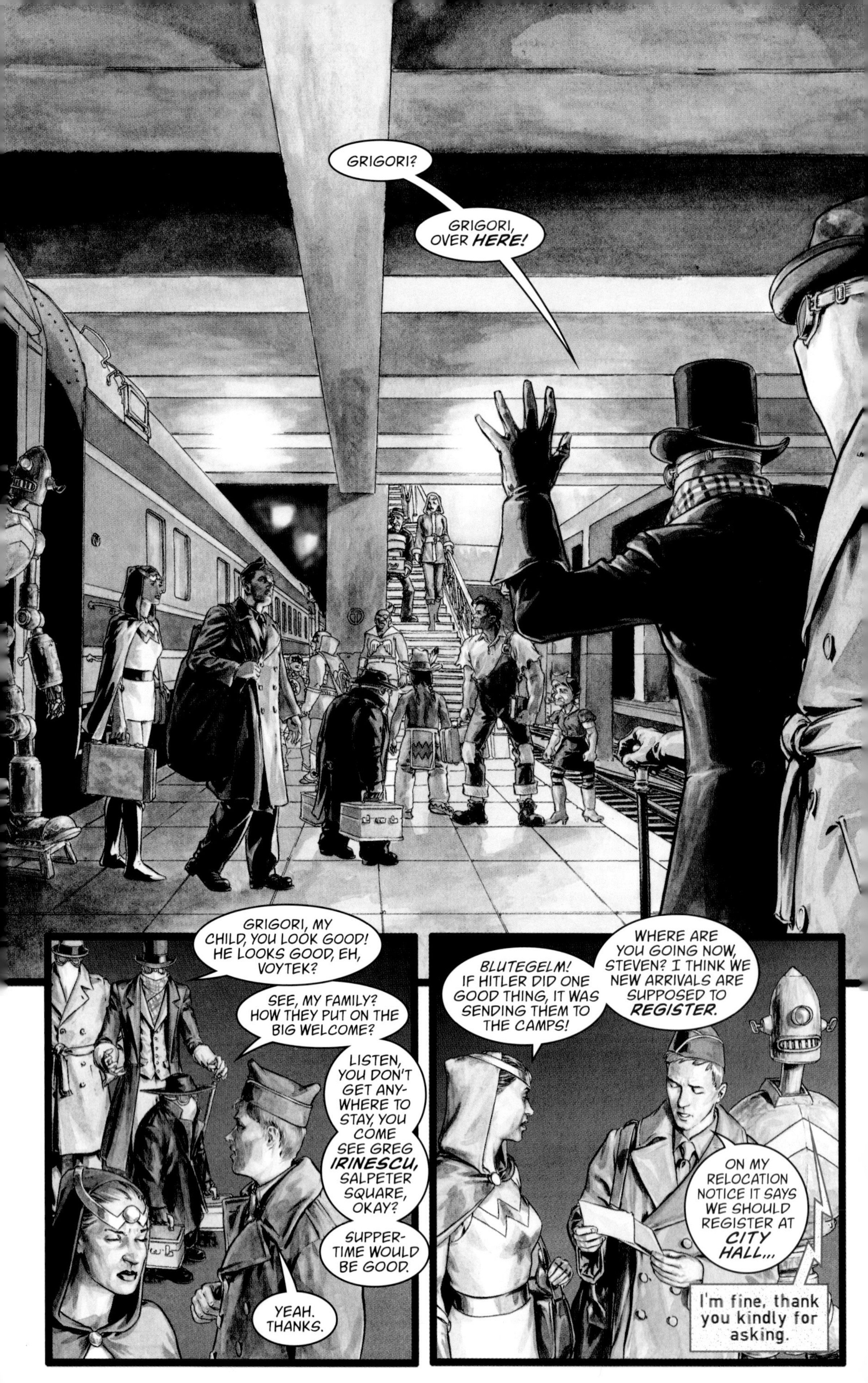
GRIGORI?
GRIGORI, OVER HERE!
GRIGORI, MY CHILD, YOU LOOK GOOD! HE LOOKS GOOD, EH, VOYTEK?
SEE, MY FAMILY? HOW THEY PUT ON THE BIG WELCOME?
LISTEN, YOU DON'T GET ANYWHERE TO STAY, YOU COME SEE GREG IRINESCU, SALPETER SQUARE, OKAY?
SUPPER-TIME WOULD BE GOOD.
YEAH. THANKS.
BLUTEGELM! IF HITLER DID ONE GOOD THING, IT WAS SENDING THEM TO THE CAMPS!
WHERE ARE YOU GOING NOW, STEVEN? I THINK WE NEW ARRIVALS ARE SUPPOSED TO REGISTER.
ON MY RELOCATION NOTICE IT SAYS WE SHOULD REGISTER AT CITY HALL...
I'm fine, thank you kindly for asking.

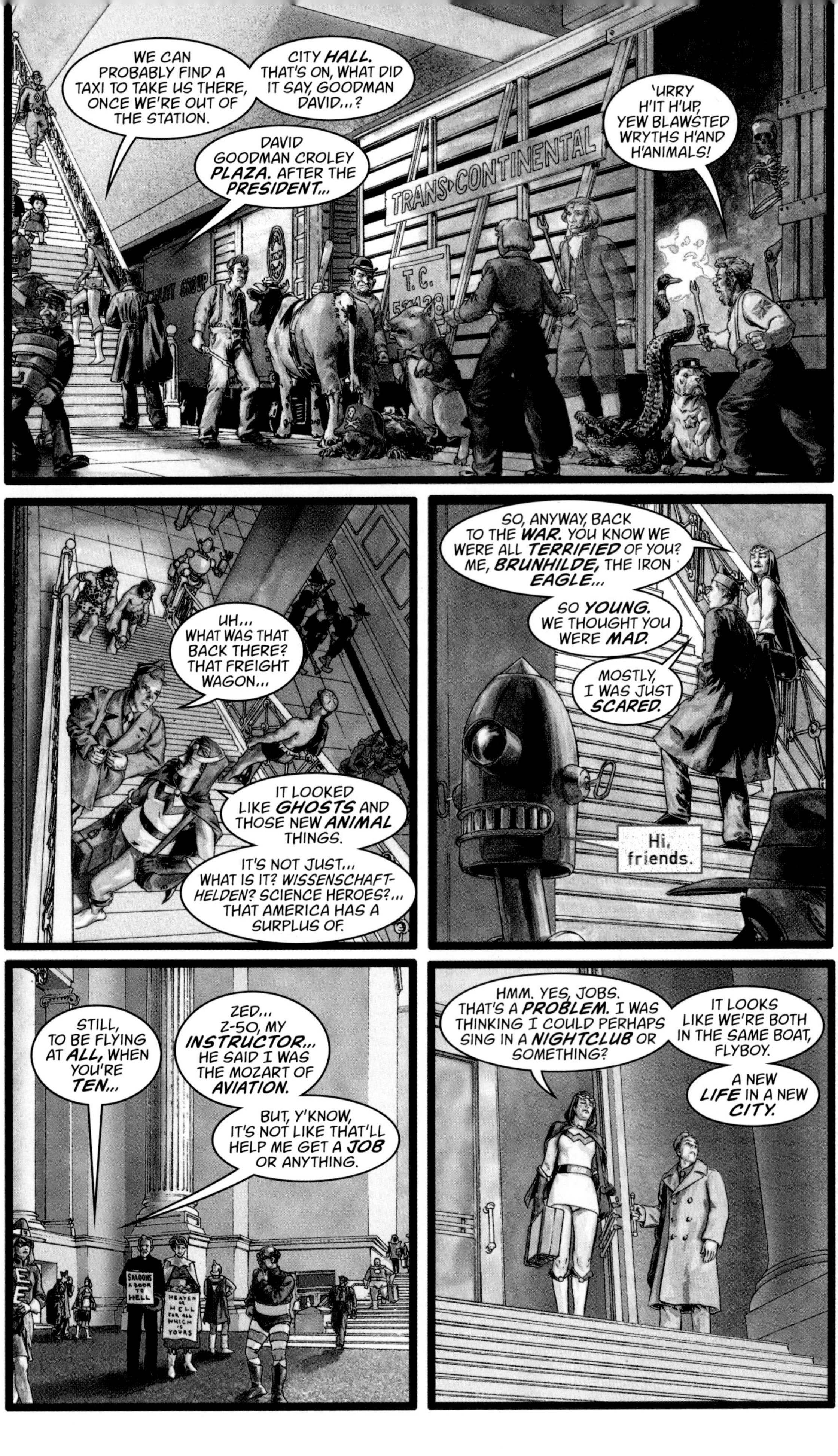
WE CAN PROBABLY FIND A TAXI TO TAKE US THERE, ONCE WE'RE OUT OF THE STATION.
CITY HALL. THAT'S ON, WHAT DID IT SAY, GOODMAN DAVID...?
DAVID GOODMAN CROLEY PLAZA. AFTER THE PRESIDENT...
TRANS CONTINENTAL
'URRY H'IT H'UP, YEW BLAWSTED WRYTHS H'AND H'ANIMALS!
UH... WHAT WAS THAT BACK THERE? THAT FREIGHT WAGON...
IT LOOKED LIKE GHOSTS AND THOSE NEW ANIMAL THINGS.
IT'S NOT JUST... WHAT IS IT? WISSENSCHAFT-HELDEN? SCIENCE HEROES?... THAT AMERICA HAS A SURPLUS OF.
SO, ANYWAY, BACK TO THE WAR. YOU KNOW WE WERE ALL TERRIFIED OF YOU? ME, BRUNHILDE, THE IRON EAGLE...
SO YOUNG. WE THOUGHT YOU WERE MAD.
MOSTLY, I WAS JUST SCARED.
Hi, friends.
STILL, TO BE FLYING AT ALL, WHEN YOU'RE TEN...
ZED... Z-50, MY INSTRUCTOR... HE SAID I WAS THE MOZART OF AVIATION.
BUT, Y'KNOW, IT'S NOT LIKE THAT'LL HELP ME GET A JOB OR ANYTHING.
HMM. YES, JOBS. THAT'S A PROBLEM. I WAS THINKING I COULD PERHAPS SING IN A NIGHTCLUB OR SOMETHING?
IT LOOKS LIKE WE'RE BOTH IN THE SAME BOAT, FLYBOY.
A NEW LIFE IN A NEW CITY.

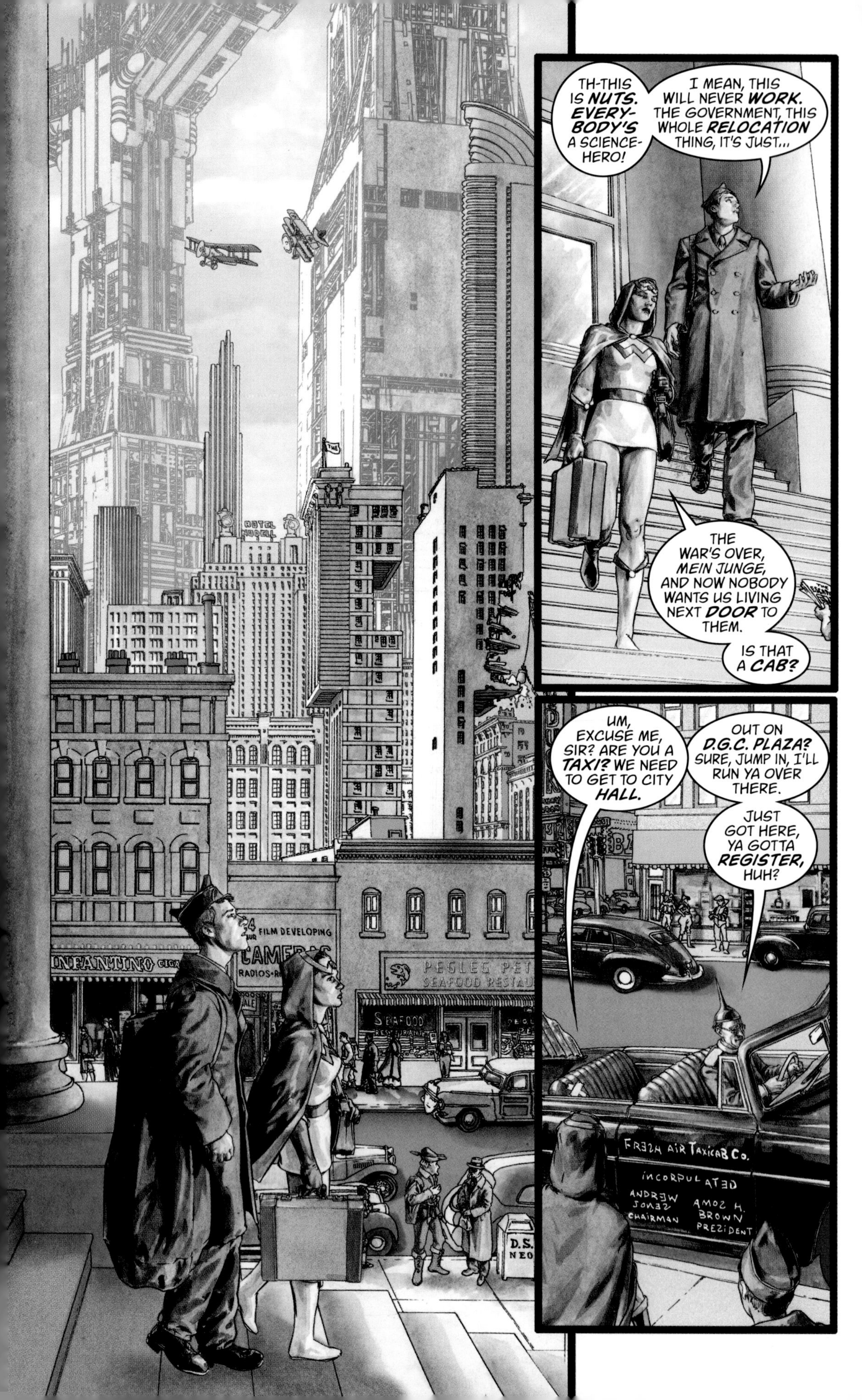
TH-THIS IS NUTS. EVERY-BODY'S A SCIENCE-HERO!
I MEAN, THIS WILL NEVER WORK. THE GOVERNMENT, THIS WHOLE RELOCATION THING, IT'S JUST...
THE WAR'S OVER, MEIN JUNGE, AND NOW NOBODY WANTS US LIVING NEXT DOOR TO THEM.
IS THAT A CAB?
UM, EXCUSE ME, SIR? ARE YOU A TAXI? WE NEED TO GET TO CITY HALL.
OUT ON D.G.C. PLAZA? SURE, JUMP IN, I'LL RUN YA OVER THERE.
JUST GOT HERE, YA GOTTA REGISTER, HUH?
FILM DEVELOPING
CAMERAS
SEAFOOD
FRESH AIR TAXICAB CO.
INCORPULATED
ANDREW JONES CHAIRMAN
AMOS H. BROWN PREZIDENT

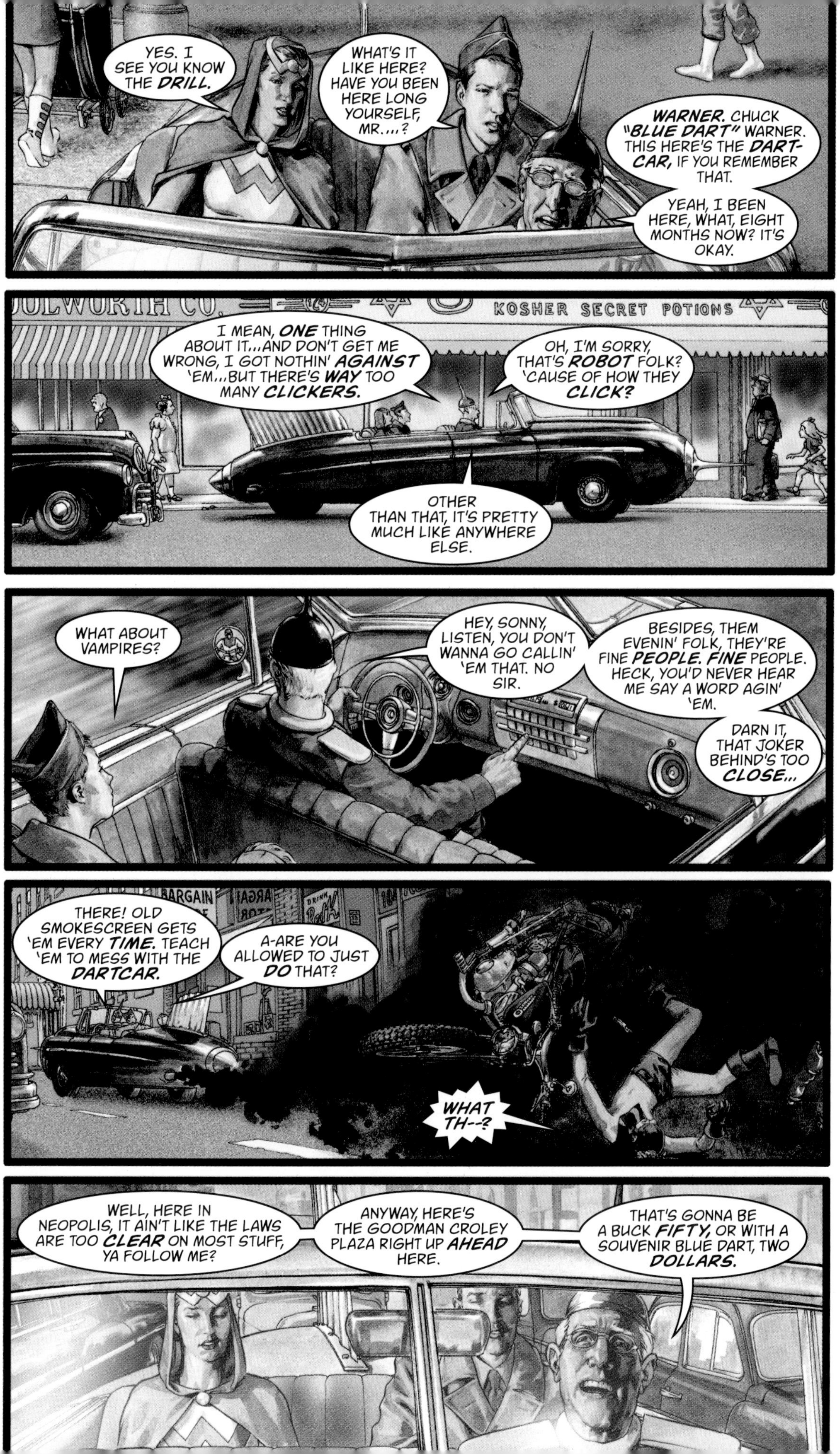
YES. I SEE YOU KNOW THE DRILL.
WHAT'S IT LIKE HERE? HAVE YOU BEEN HERE LONG YOURSELF, MR....?
WARNER. CHUCK "BLUE DART" WARNER. THIS HERE'S THE DART-CAR, IF YOU REMEMBER THAT.
YEAH, I BEEN HERE, WHAT, EIGHT MONTHS NOW? IT'S OKAY.
KOSHER SECRET POTIONS
I MEAN, ONE THING ABOUT IT...AND DON'T GET ME WRONG, I GOT NOTHIN' AGAINST 'EM...BUT THERE'S WAY TOO MANY CLICKERS.
OH, I'M SORRY, THAT'S ROBOT FOLK? 'CAUSE OF HOW THEY CLICK?
OTHER THAN THAT, IT'S PRETTY MUCH LIKE ANYWHERE ELSE.
WHAT ABOUT VAMPIRES?
HEY, SONNY, LISTEN, YOU DON'T WANNA GO CALLIN' 'EM THAT. NO SIR.
BESIDES, THEM EVENIN' FOLK, THEY'RE FINE PEOPLE. FINE PEOPLE. HECK, YOU'D NEVER HEAR ME SAY A WORD AGIN' 'EM.
DARN IT, THAT JOKER BEHIND'S TOO CLOSE...
BARGAIN
THERE! OLD SMOKESCREEN GETS 'EM EVERY TIME. TEACH 'EM TO MESS WITH THE DARTCAR.
A-ARE YOU ALLOWED TO JUST DO THAT?
WHAT TH--?
WELL, HERE IN NEOPOLIS, IT AIN'T LIKE THE LAWS ARE TOO CLEAR ON MOST STUFF, YA FOLLOW ME?
ANYWAY, HERE'S THE GOODMAN CROLEY PLAZA RIGHT UP AHEAD HERE.
THAT'S GONNA BE A BUCK FIFTY, OR WITH A SOUVENIR BLUE DART, TWO DOLLARS.

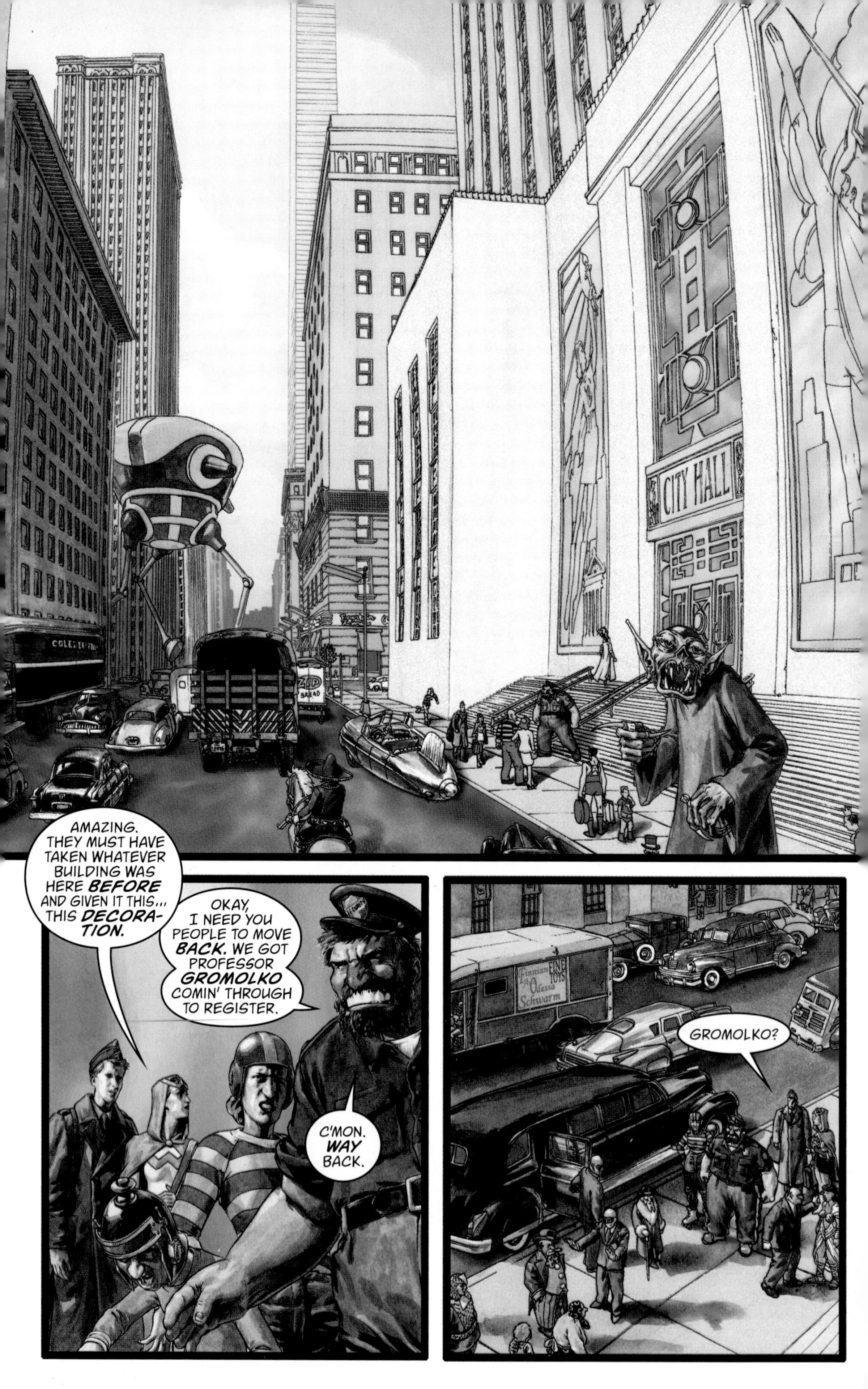
CITY HALL
ZIP BREAD
AMAZING. THEY MUST HAVE TAKEN WHATEVER BUILDING WAS HERE *BEFORE* AND GIVEN IT THIS... THIS *DECORATION.*
OKAY, I NEED YOU PEOPLE TO MOVE *BACK.* WE GOT PROFESSOR *GROMOLKO* COMIN' THROUGH TO REGISTER.
C'MON. *WAY* BACK.
Finnian & Odessa Schwarm FINE TOYS
GROMOLKO?

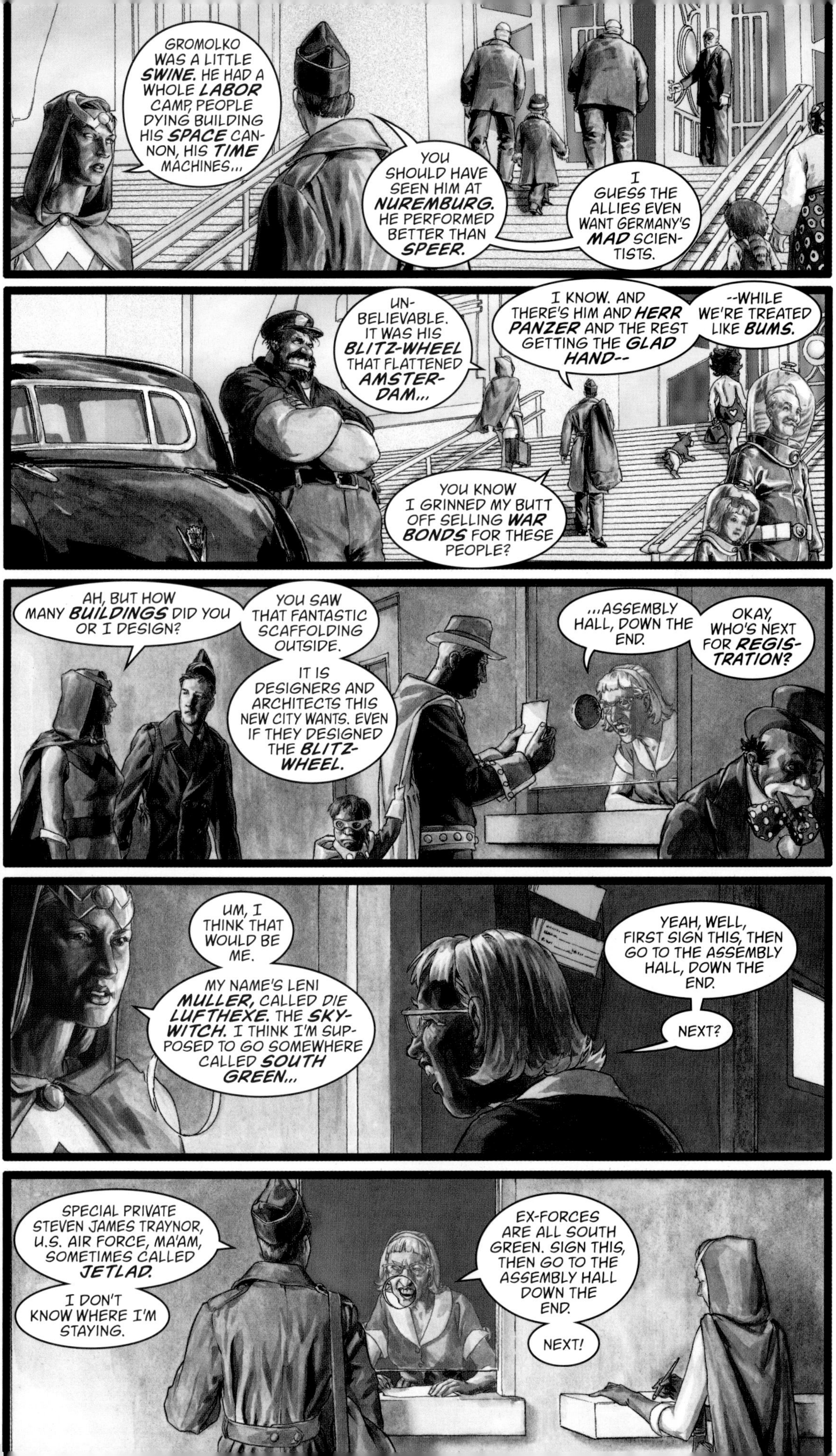
GROMOLKO WAS A LITTLE SWINE. HE HAD A WHOLE LABOR CAMP, PEOPLE DYING BUILDING HIS SPACE CANNON, HIS TIME MACHINES...
YOU SHOULD HAVE SEEN HIM AT NUREMBURG. HE PERFORMED BETTER THAN SPEER.
I GUESS THE ALLIES EVEN WANT GERMANY'S MAD SCIENTISTS.
UNBELIEVABLE. IT WAS HIS BLITZ-WHEEL THAT FLATTENED AMSTERDAM...
I KNOW. AND THERE'S HIM AND HERR PANZER AND THE REST GETTING THE GLAD HAND--
--WHILE WE'RE TREATED LIKE BUMS.
YOU KNOW I GRINNED MY BUTT OFF SELLING WAR BONDS FOR THESE PEOPLE?
AH, BUT HOW MANY BUILDINGS DID YOU OR I DESIGN?
YOU SAW THAT FANTASTIC SCAFFOLDING OUTSIDE.
IT IS DESIGNERS AND ARCHITECTS THIS NEW CITY WANTS. EVEN IF THEY DESIGNED THE BLITZ-WHEEL.
...ASSEMBLY HALL, DOWN THE END.
OKAY, WHO'S NEXT FOR REGISTRATION?
UM, I THINK THAT WOULD BE ME.
MY NAME'S LENI MULLER, CALLED DIE LUFTHEXE. THE SKY-WITCH. I THINK I'M SUPPOSED TO GO SOMEWHERE CALLED SOUTH GREEN...
YEAH, WELL, FIRST SIGN THIS, THEN GO TO THE ASSEMBLY HALL, DOWN THE END.
NEXT?
SPECIAL PRIVATE STEVEN JAMES TRAYNOR, U.S. AIR FORCE, MA'AM, SOMETIMES CALLED JETLAD.
I DON'T KNOW WHERE I'M STAYING.
EX-FORCES ARE ALL SOUTH GREEN. SIGN THIS, THEN GO TO THE ASSEMBLY HALL DOWN THE END.
NEXT!

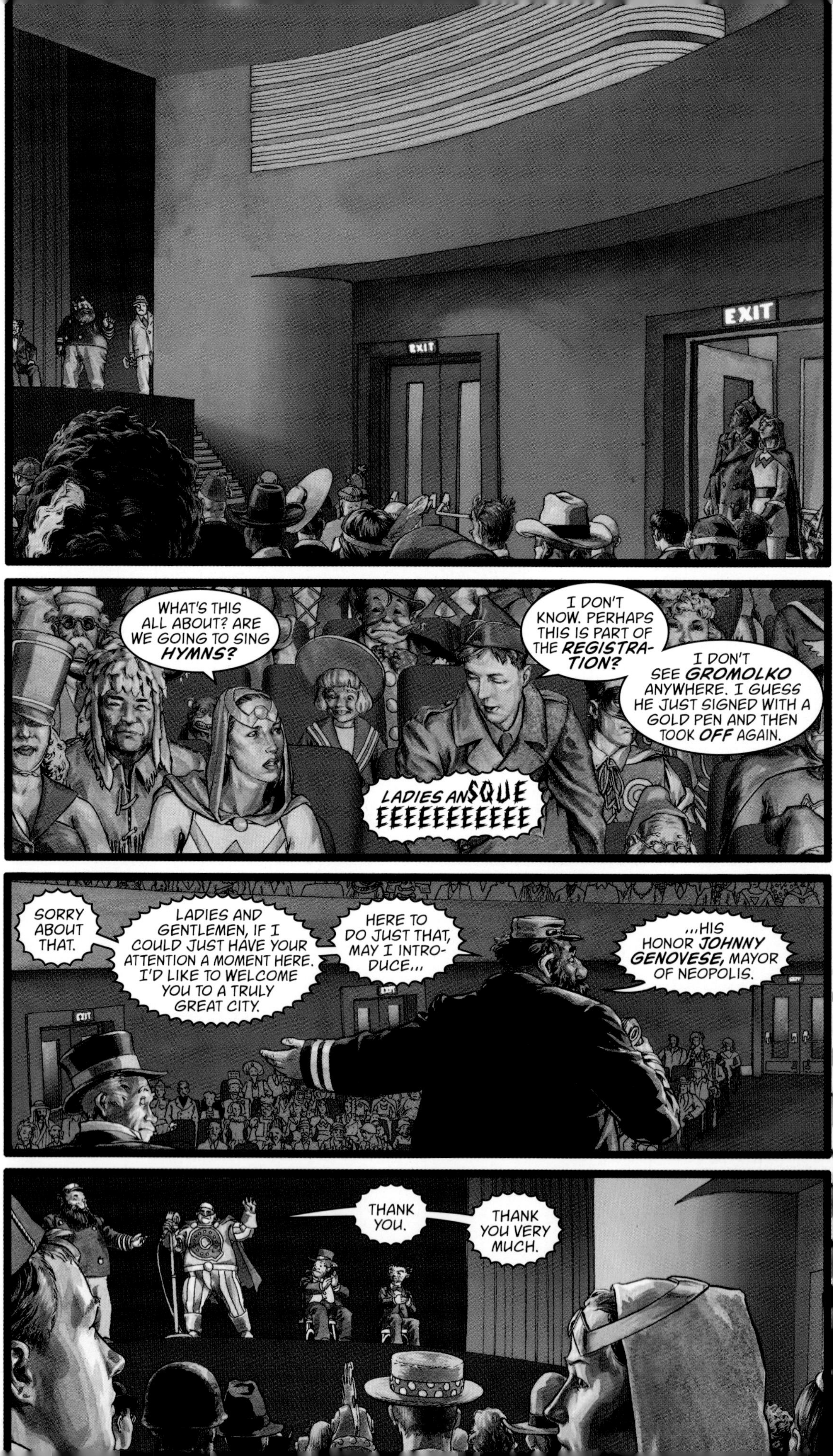
EXIT
EXIT
WHAT'S THIS ALL ABOUT? ARE WE GOING TO SING HYMNS?
I DON'T KNOW. PERHAPS THIS IS PART OF THE REGISTRATION?
I DON'T SEE GROMOLKO ANYWHERE. I GUESS HE JUST SIGNED WITH A GOLD PEN AND THEN TOOK OFF AGAIN.
LADIES ANSQUE EEEEEEEEEEE
SORRY ABOUT THAT.
LADIES AND GENTLEMEN, IF I COULD JUST HAVE YOUR ATTENTION A MOMENT HERE. I'D LIKE TO WELCOME YOU TO A TRULY GREAT CITY.
HERE TO DO JUST THAT, MAY I INTRODUCE...
...HIS HONOR JOHNNY GENOVESE, MAYOR OF NEOPOLIS.
THANK YOU.
THANK YOU VERY MUCH.

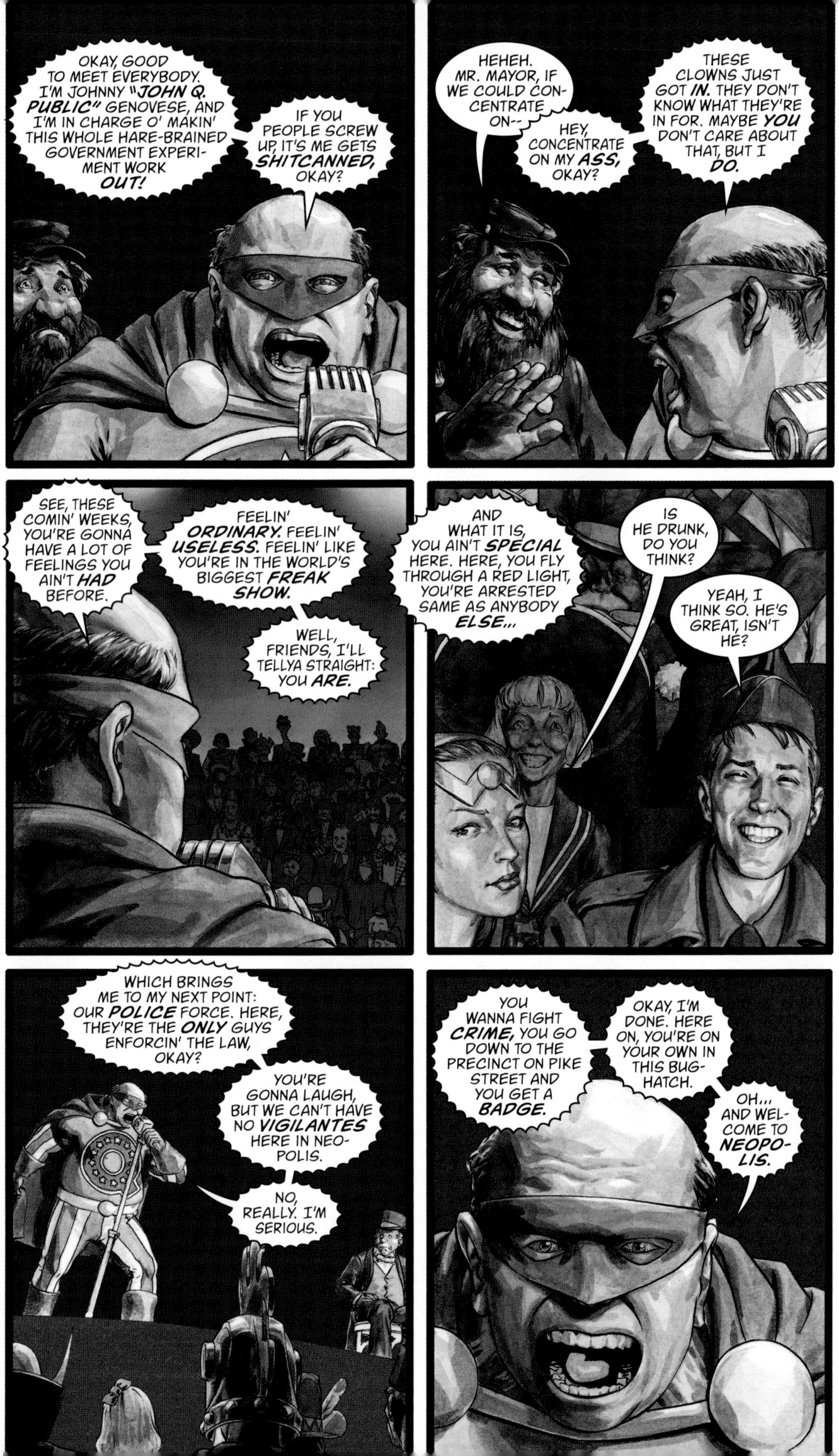
OKAY, GOOD TO MEET EVERYBODY. I'M JOHNNY "JOHN Q. PUBLIC" GENOVESE, AND I'M IN CHARGE O' MAKIN' THIS WHOLE HARE-BRAINED GOVERNMENT EXPERIMENT WORK OUT!
IF YOU PEOPLE SCREW UP, IT'S ME GETS SHITCANNED, OKAY?
HEHEH. MR. MAYOR, IF WE COULD CONCENTRATE ON--
HEY, CONCENTRATE ON MY ASS, OKAY?
THESE CLOWNS JUST GOT IN. THEY DON'T KNOW WHAT THEY'RE IN FOR. MAYBE YOU DON'T CARE ABOUT THAT, BUT I DO.
SEE, THESE COMIN' WEEKS, YOU'RE GONNA HAVE A LOT OF FEELINGS YOU AIN'T HAD BEFORE.
FEELIN' ORDINARY. FEELIN' USELESS. FEELIN' LIKE YOU'RE IN THE WORLD'S BIGGEST FREAK SHOW.
WELL, FRIENDS, I'LL TELLYA STRAIGHT: YOU ARE.
AND WHAT IT IS, YOU AIN'T SPECIAL HERE. HERE, YOU FLY THROUGH A RED LIGHT, YOU'RE ARRESTED SAME AS ANYBODY ELSE...
IS HE DRUNK, DO YOU THINK?
YEAH, I THINK SO. HE'S GREAT, ISN'T HE?
WHICH BRINGS ME TO MY NEXT POINT: OUR POLICE FORCE. HERE, THEY'RE THE ONLY GUYS ENFORCIN' THE LAW, OKAY?
YOU'RE GONNA LAUGH, BUT WE CAN'T HAVE NO VIGILANTES HERE IN NEOPOLIS.
NO, REALLY. I'M SERIOUS.
YOU WANNA FIGHT CRIME, YOU GO DOWN TO THE PRECINCT ON PIKE STREET AND YOU GET A BADGE.
OKAY, I'M DONE. HERE ON, YOU'RE ON YOUR OWN IN THIS BUG-HATCH.
OH... AND WELCOME TO NEOPOLIS.

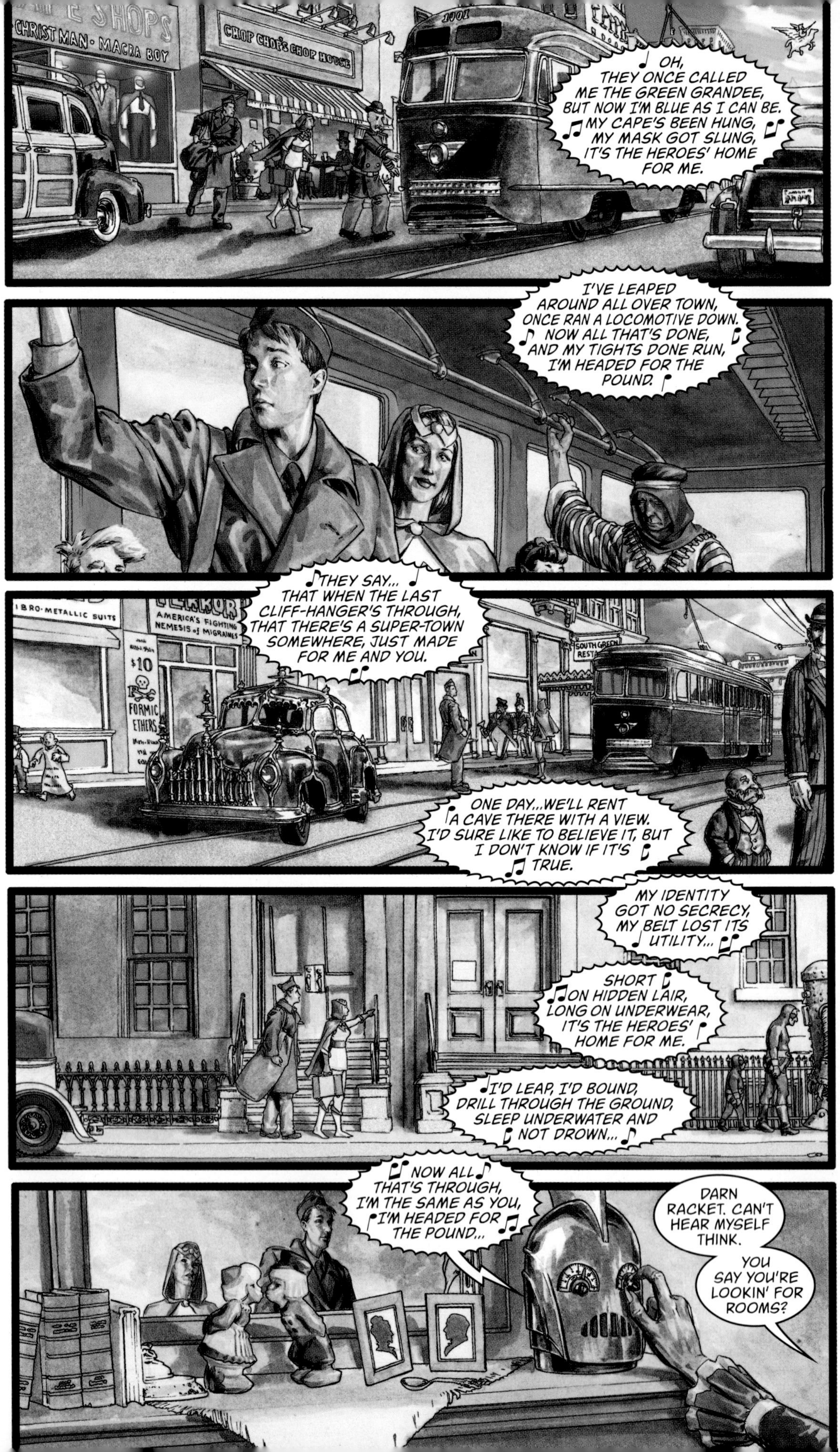
CHRIST MAN · MACRA BOY
CHOP CHOP'S CHOP HOUSE
OH, THEY ONCE CALLED ME THE GREEN GRANDEE, BUT NOW I'M BLUE AS I CAN BE. MY CAPE'S BEEN HUNG, MY MASK GOT SLUNG, IT'S THE HEROES' HOME FOR ME.
I'VE LEAPED AROUND ALL OVER TOWN, ONCE RAN A LOCOMOTIVE DOWN. NOW ALL THAT'S DONE, AND MY TIGHTS DONE RUN, I'M HEADED FOR THE POUND.
THEY SAY... THAT WHEN THE LAST CLIFF-HANGER'S THROUGH, THAT THERE'S A SUPER-TOWN SOMEWHERE, JUST MADE FOR ME AND YOU.
IBRO-METALLIC SUITS
AMERICA'S FIGHTING NEMESIS of MIGRAINES
$10
FORMIC ETHERS
SOUTH GREEN RESTA
ONE DAY...WE'LL RENT A CAVE THERE WITH A VIEW. I'D SURE LIKE TO BELIEVE IT, BUT I DON'T KNOW IF IT'S TRUE.
MY IDENTITY GOT NO SECRECY, MY BELT LOST ITS UTILITY...
SHORT ON HIDDEN LAIR, LONG ON UNDERWEAR, IT'S THE HEROES' HOME FOR ME.
I'D LEAP, I'D BOUND, DRILL THROUGH THE GROUND, SLEEP UNDERWATER AND NOT DROWN...
NOW ALL THAT'S THROUGH, I'M THE SAME AS YOU, I'M HEADED FOR THE POUND...
DARN RACKET. CAN'T HEAR MYSELF THINK.
YOU SAY YOU'RE LOOKIN' FOR ROOMS?

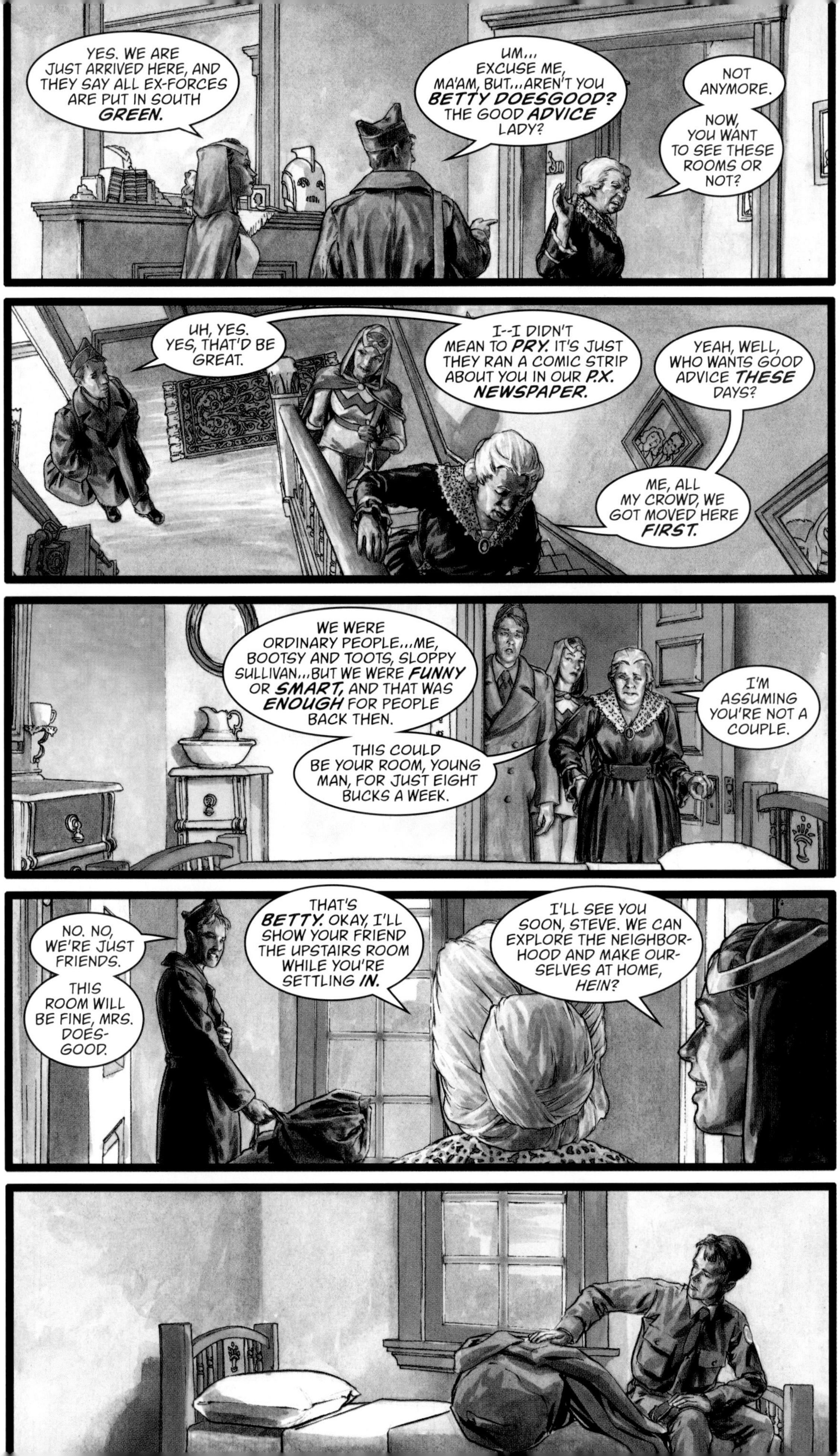
YES. WE ARE JUST ARRIVED HERE, AND THEY SAY ALL EX-FORCES ARE PUT IN SOUTH **GREEN.**
UM... EXCUSE ME, MA'AM, BUT...AREN'T YOU **BETTY DOESGOOD?** THE GOOD **ADVICE** LADY?
NOT ANYMORE.
NOW, YOU WANT TO SEE THESE ROOMS OR NOT?
UH, YES. YES, THAT'D BE GREAT.
I--I DIDN'T MEAN TO **PRY.** IT'S JUST THEY RAN A COMIC STRIP ABOUT YOU IN OUR **P.X. NEWSPAPER.**
YEAH, WELL, WHO WANTS GOOD ADVICE **THESE** DAYS?
ME, ALL MY CROWD, WE GOT MOVED HERE **FIRST.**
WE WERE ORDINARY PEOPLE...ME, BOOTSY AND TOOTS, SLOPPY SULLIVAN...BUT WE WERE **FUNNY** OR **SMART,** AND THAT WAS **ENOUGH** FOR PEOPLE BACK THEN.
THIS COULD BE YOUR ROOM, YOUNG MAN, FOR JUST EIGHT BUCKS A WEEK.
I'M ASSUMING YOU'RE NOT A COUPLE.
NO. NO, WE'RE JUST FRIENDS.
THIS ROOM WILL BE FINE, MRS. DOES-GOOD.
THAT'S **BETTY.** OKAY, I'LL SHOW YOUR FRIEND THE UPSTAIRS ROOM WHILE YOU'RE SETTLING **IN.**
I'LL SEE YOU SOON, STEVE. WE CAN EXPLORE THE NEIGHBOR-HOOD AND MAKE OUR-SELVES AT HOME, HEIN?

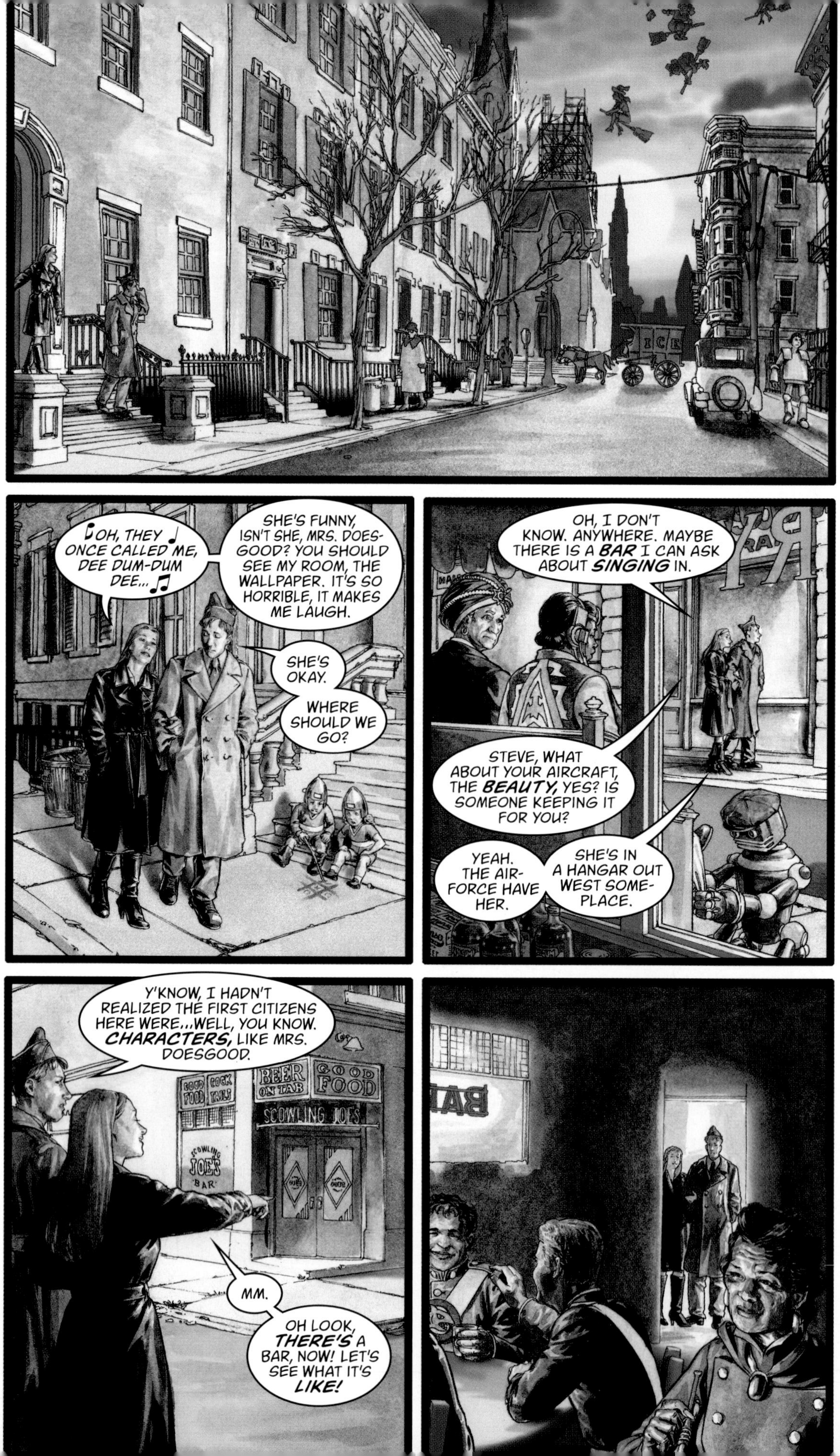
ICE
OH, THEY ONCE CALLED ME, DEE DUM-DUM DEE...
SHE'S FUNNY, ISN'T SHE, MRS. DOES-GOOD? YOU SHOULD SEE MY ROOM, THE WALLPAPER. IT'S SO HORRIBLE, IT MAKES ME LAUGH.
SHE'S OKAY.
WHERE SHOULD WE GO?
OH, I DON'T KNOW. ANYWHERE. MAYBE THERE IS A **BAR** I CAN ASK ABOUT **SINGING** IN.
STEVE, WHAT ABOUT YOUR AIRCRAFT, THE **BEAUTY,** YES? IS SOMEONE KEEPING IT FOR YOU?
YEAH. THE AIR-FORCE HAVE HER.
SHE'S IN A HANGAR OUT WEST SOME-PLACE.
Y'KNOW, I HADN'T REALIZED THE FIRST CITIZENS HERE WERE...WELL, YOU KNOW. **CHARACTERS,** LIKE MRS. DOESGOOD.
GOOD FOOD
COCK TAILS
BEER ON TAB
GOOD FOOD
SCOWLING JOES
SCOWLING JOE'S BAR
MM.
OH LOOK, **THERE'S** A BAR, NOW! LET'S SEE WHAT IT'S **LIKE!**

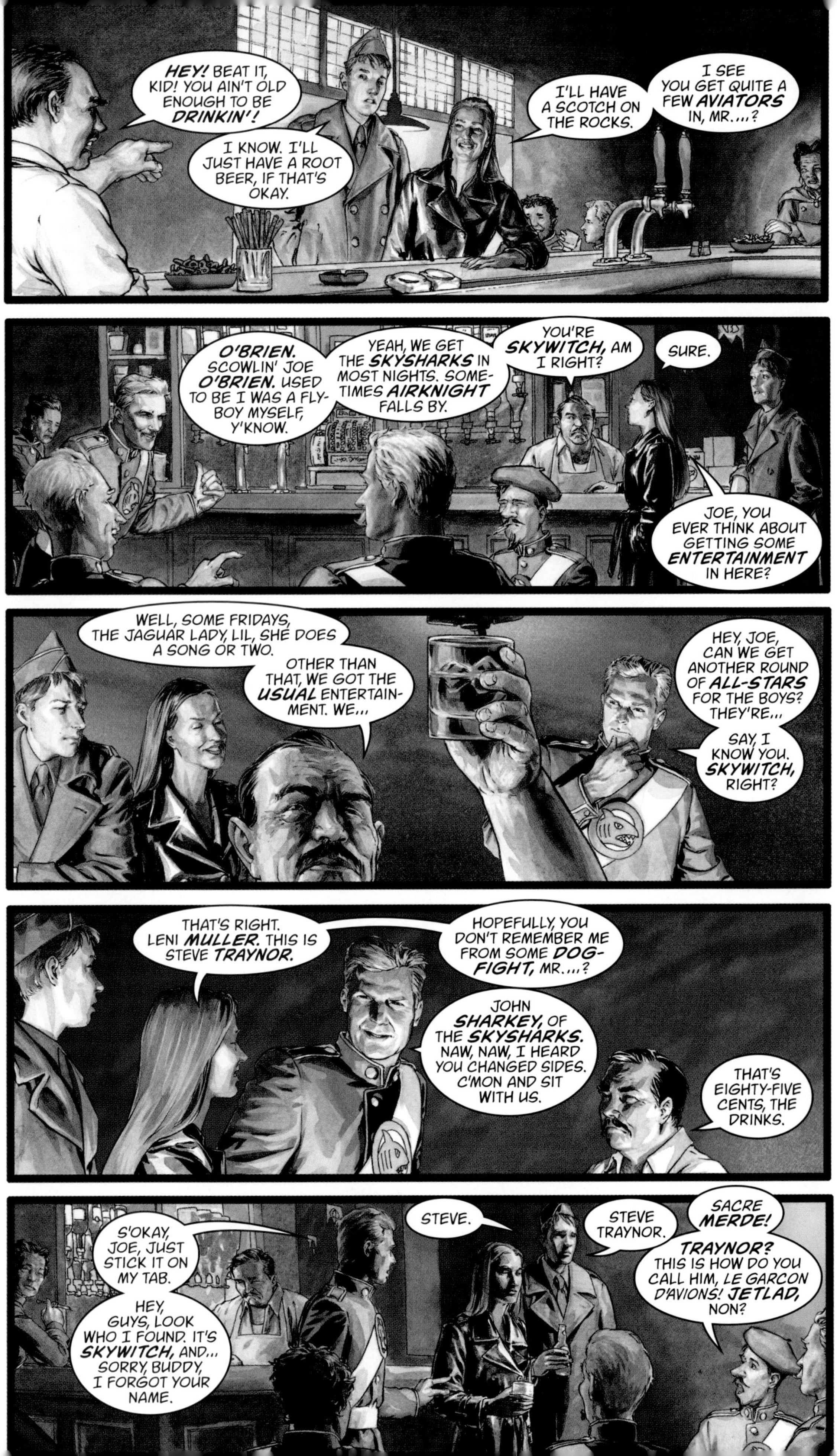
HEY! BEAT IT, KID! YOU AIN'T OLD ENOUGH TO BE DRINKIN'!
I KNOW. I'LL JUST HAVE A ROOT BEER, IF THAT'S OKAY.
I'LL HAVE A SCOTCH ON THE ROCKS.
I SEE YOU GET QUITE A FEW AVIATORS IN, MR....?
O'BRIEN. SCOWLIN' JOE O'BRIEN. USED TO BE I WAS A FLY-BOY MYSELF, Y'KNOW.
YEAH, WE GET THE SKYSHARKS IN MOST NIGHTS. SOMETIMES AIRKNIGHT FALLS BY.
YOU'RE SKYWITCH, AM I RIGHT?
SURE.
JOE, YOU EVER THINK ABOUT GETTING SOME ENTERTAINMENT IN HERE?
WELL, SOME FRIDAYS, THE JAGUAR LADY, LIL, SHE DOES A SONG OR TWO.
OTHER THAN THAT, WE GOT THE USUAL ENTERTAINMENT. WE...
HEY, JOE, CAN WE GET ANOTHER ROUND OF ALL-STARS FOR THE BOYS? THEY'RE...
SAY, I KNOW YOU. SKYWITCH, RIGHT?
THAT'S RIGHT. LENI MULLER. THIS IS STEVE TRAYNOR.
HOPEFULLY, YOU DON'T REMEMBER ME FROM SOME DOGFIGHT, MR....?
JOHN SHARKEY, OF THE SKYSHARKS. NAW, NAW, I HEARD YOU CHANGED SIDES. C'MON AND SIT WITH US.
THAT'S EIGHTY-FIVE CENTS, THE DRINKS.
S'OKAY, JOE, JUST STICK IT ON MY TAB.
HEY, GUYS, LOOK WHO I FOUND. IT'S SKYWITCH, AND... SORRY, BUDDY, I FORGOT YOUR NAME.
STEVE.
STEVE TRAYNOR.
SACRE MERDE!
TRAYNOR? THIS IS HOW DO YOU CALL HIM, LE GARCON D'AVIONS! JETLAD, NON?

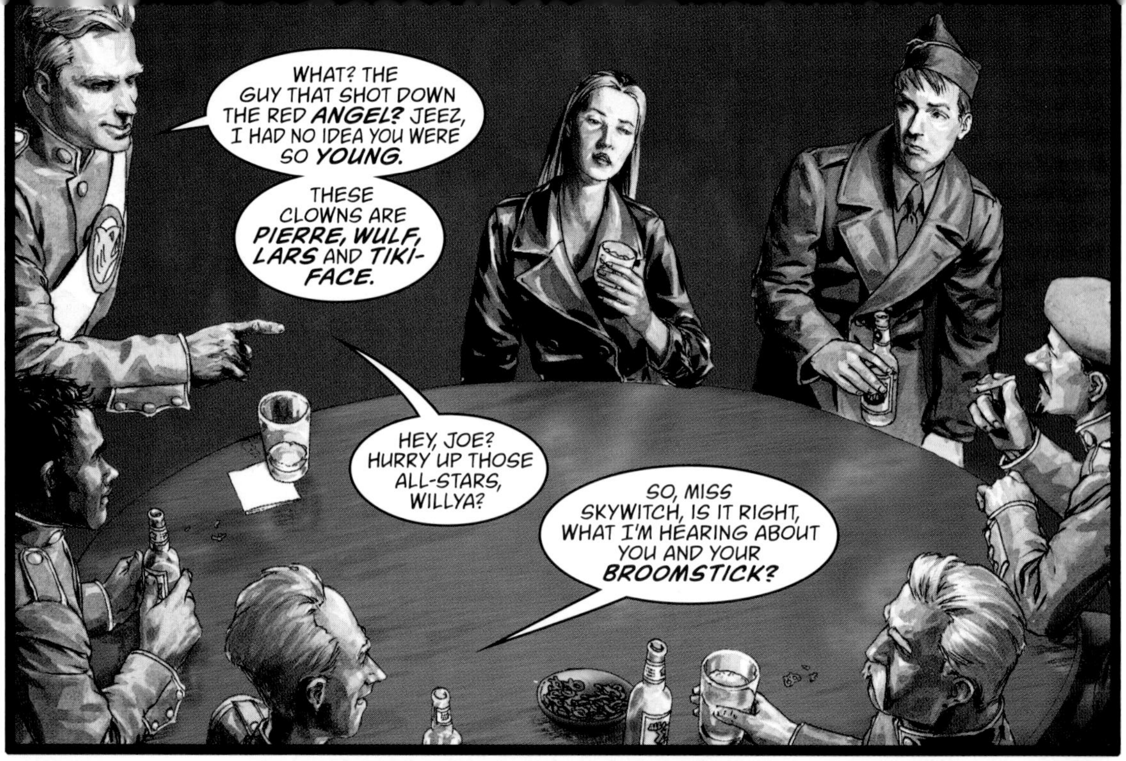
WHAT? THE GUY THAT SHOT DOWN THE RED ANGEL? JEEZ, I HAD NO IDEA YOU WERE SO YOUNG.
THESE CLOWNS ARE PIERRE, WULF, LARS AND TIKI-FACE.
HEY, JOE? HURRY UP THOSE ALL-STARS, WILLYA?
SO, MISS SKYWITCH, IS IT RIGHT, WHAT I'M HEARING ABOUT YOU AND YOUR BROOMSTICK?

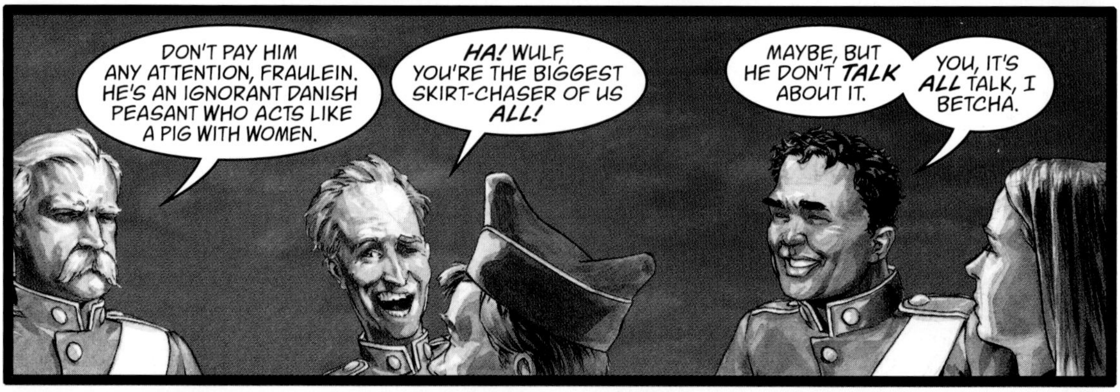
DON'T PAY HIM ANY ATTENTION, FRAULEIN. HE'S AN IGNORANT DANISH PEASANT WHO ACTS LIKE A PIG WITH WOMEN.
HA! WULF, YOU'RE THE BIGGEST SKIRT-CHASER OF US ALL!
MAYBE, BUT HE DON'T TALK ABOUT IT.
YOU, IT'S ALL TALK, I BETCHA.

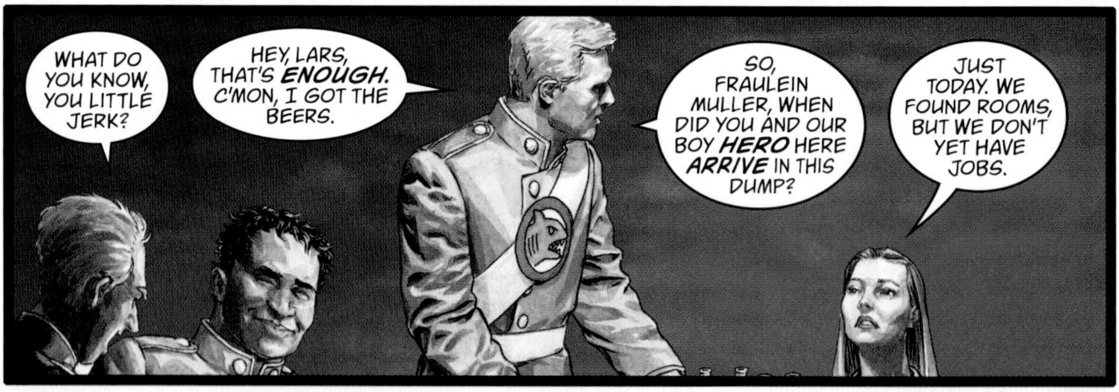
WHAT DO YOU KNOW, YOU LITTLE JERK?
HEY, LARS, THAT'S ENOUGH. C'MON, I GOT THE BEERS.
SO, FRAULEIN MULLER, WHEN DID YOU AND OUR BOY HERO HERE ARRIVE IN THIS DUMP?
JUST TODAY. WE FOUND ROOMS, BUT WE DON'T YET HAVE JOBS.

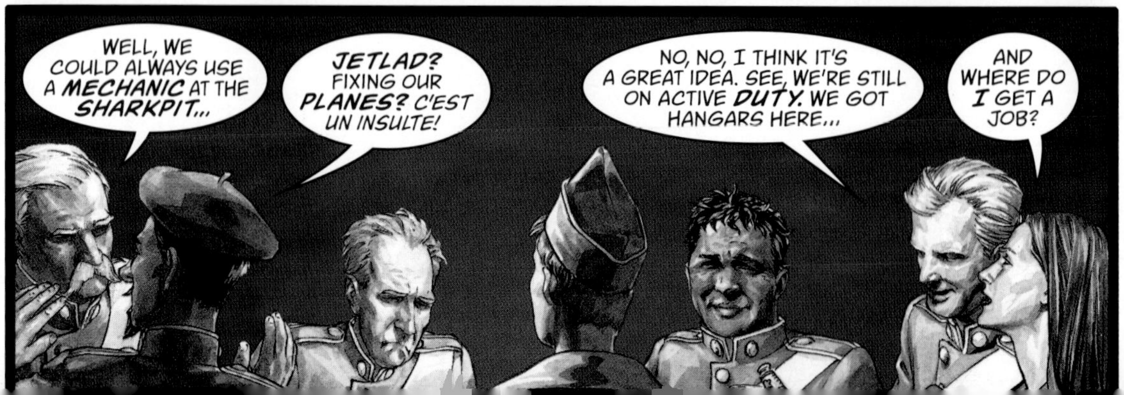
WELL, WE COULD ALWAYS USE A MECHANIC AT THE SHARKPIT...
JETLAD? FIXING OUR PLANES? C'EST UN INSULTE!
NO, NO, I THINK IT'S A GREAT IDEA. SEE, WE'RE STILL ON ACTIVE DUTY. WE GOT HANGARS HERE...
AND WHERE DO I GET A JOB?

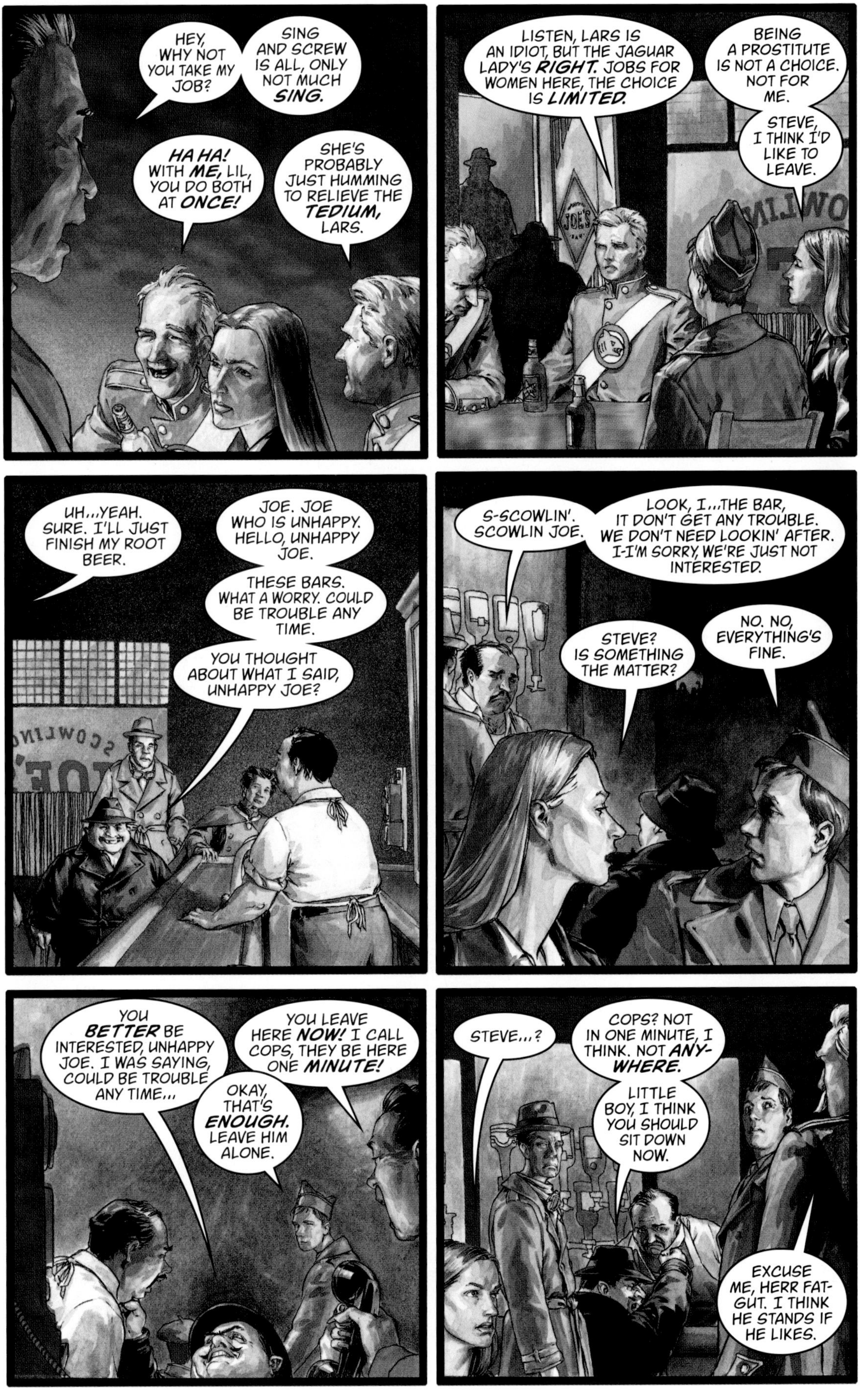
HEY, WHY NOT YOU TAKE MY JOB?
SING AND SCREW IS ALL, ONLY NOT MUCH SING.
HA HA! WITH ME, LIL, YOU DO BOTH AT ONCE!
SHE'S PROBABLY JUST HUMMING TO RELIEVE THE TEDIUM, LARS.
LISTEN, LARS IS AN IDIOT, BUT THE JAGUAR LADY'S RIGHT. JOBS FOR WOMEN HERE, THE CHOICE IS LIMITED.
BEING A PROSTITUTE IS NOT A CHOICE. NOT FOR ME.
STEVE, I THINK I'D LIKE TO LEAVE.
UH...YEAH. SURE. I'LL JUST FINISH MY ROOT BEER.
JOE. JOE WHO IS UNHAPPY. HELLO, UNHAPPY JOE.
THESE BARS. WHAT A WORRY. COULD BE TROUBLE ANY TIME.
YOU THOUGHT ABOUT WHAT I SAID, UNHAPPY JOE?
S-SCOWLIN'. SCOWLIN JOE.
LOOK, I...THE BAR, IT DON'T GET ANY TROUBLE. WE DON'T NEED LOOKIN' AFTER. I-I'M SORRY, WE'RE JUST NOT INTERESTED.
STEVE? IS SOMETHING THE MATTER?
NO. NO, EVERYTHING'S FINE.
YOU BETTER BE INTERESTED, UNHAPPY JOE. I WAS SAYING, COULD BE TROUBLE ANY TIME...
YOU LEAVE HERE NOW! I CALL COPS, THEY BE HERE ONE MINUTE!
OKAY, THAT'S ENOUGH. LEAVE HIM ALONE.
STEVE...?
COPS? NOT IN ONE MINUTE, I THINK. NOT ANY-WHERE.
LITTLE BOY, I THINK YOU SHOULD SIT DOWN NOW.
EXCUSE ME, HERR FAT-GUT. I THINK HE STANDS IF HE LIKES.

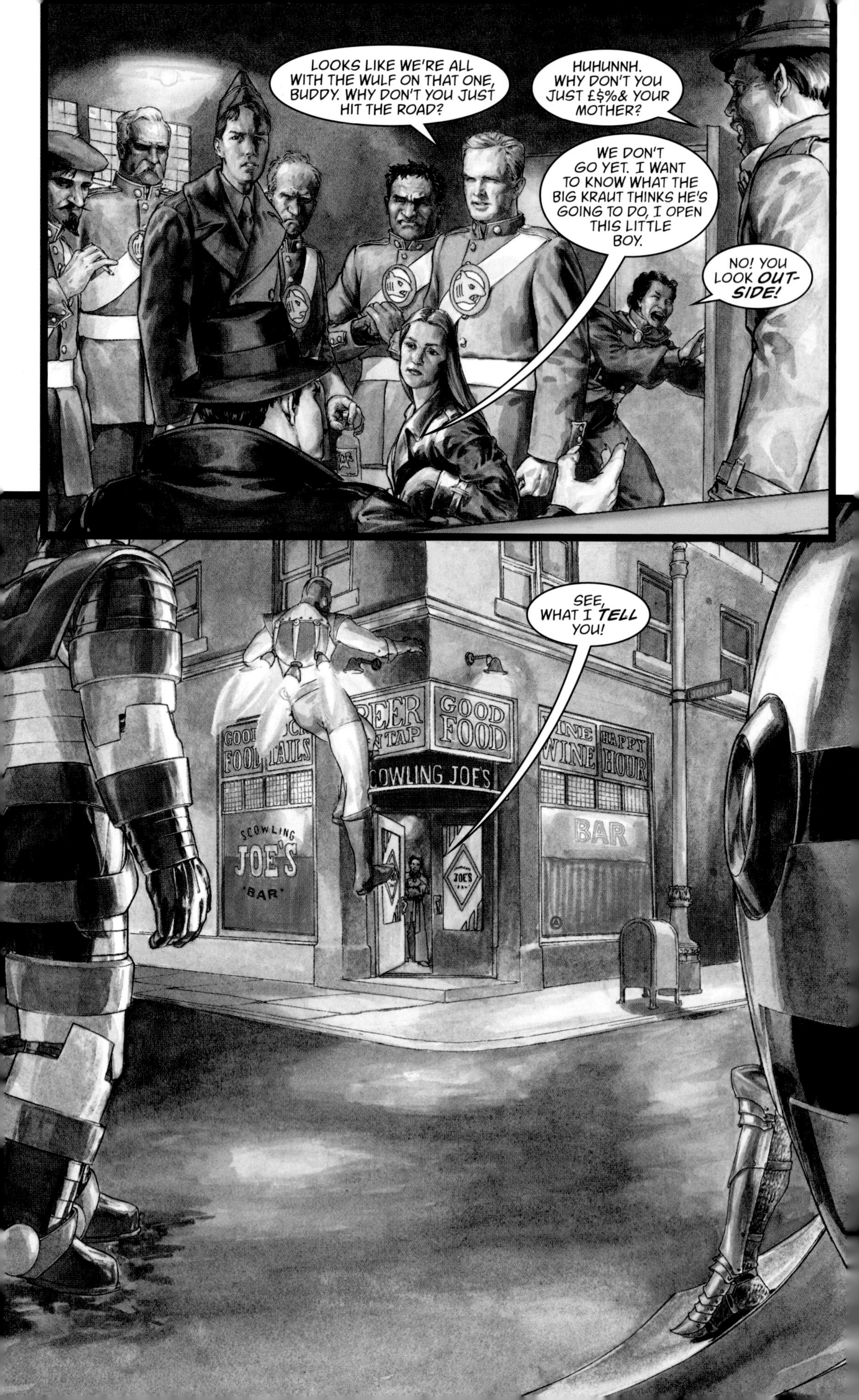
LOOKS LIKE WE'RE ALL WITH THE WULF ON THAT ONE, BUDDY. WHY DON'T YOU JUST HIT THE ROAD?
HUHUNNH. WHY DON'T YOU JUST £$%& YOUR MOTHER?
WE DON'T GO YET. I WANT TO KNOW WHAT THE BIG KRAUT THINKS HE'S GOING TO DO, I OPEN THIS LITTLE BOY.
NO! YOU LOOK OUT-SIDE!
SEE, WHAT I TELL YOU!
GOOD FOOD
HAPPY HOUR
SCOWLING JOE'S 'BAR'
JOE'S
BAR

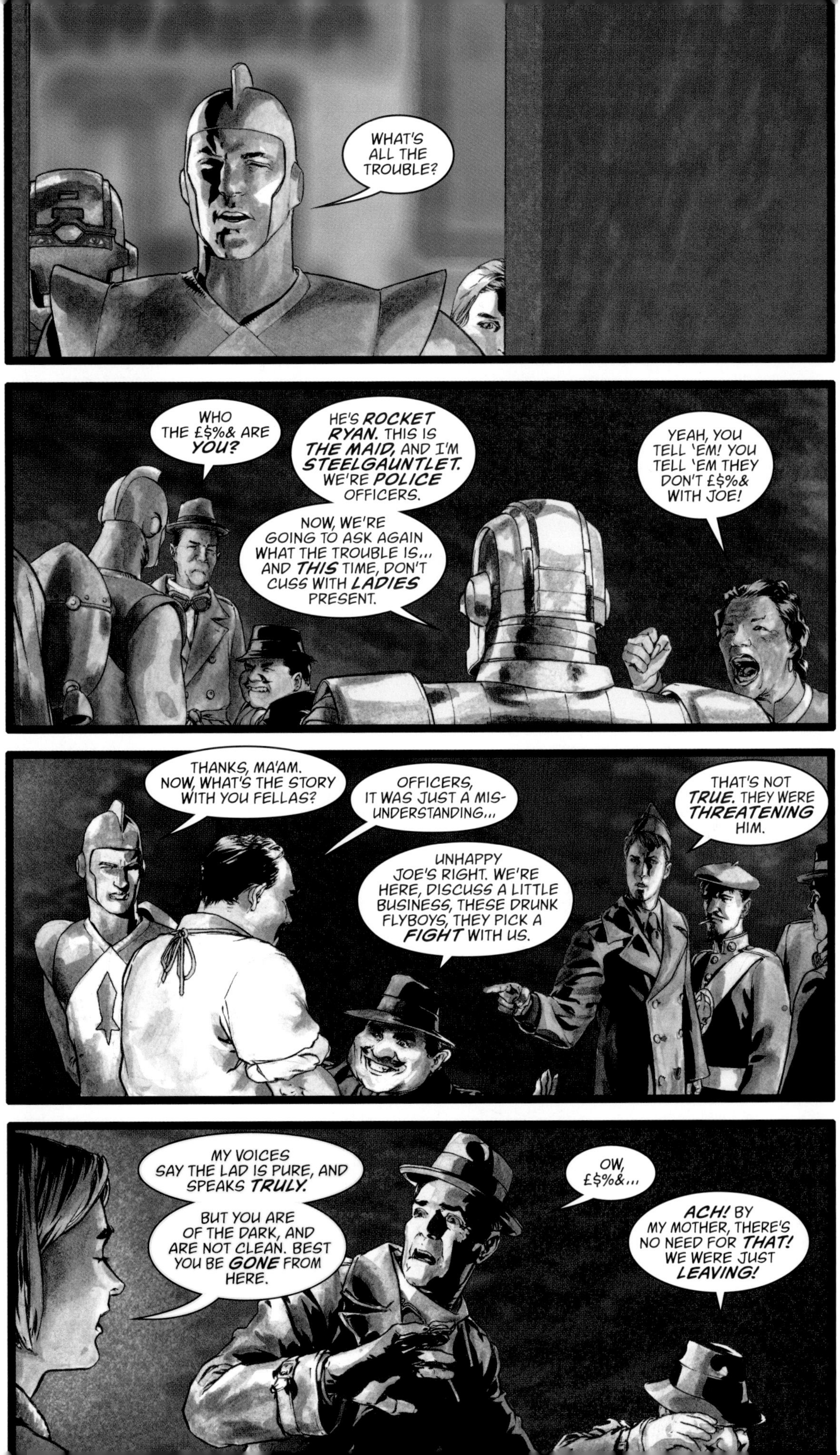
WHAT'S ALL THE TROUBLE?
WHO THE £$%& ARE YOU?
HE'S ROCKET RYAN. THIS IS THE MAID, AND I'M STEELGAUNTLET. WE'RE POLICE OFFICERS.
NOW, WE'RE GOING TO ASK AGAIN WHAT THE TROUBLE IS... AND THIS TIME, DON'T CUSS WITH LADIES PRESENT.
YEAH, YOU TELL 'EM! YOU TELL 'EM THEY DON'T £$%& WITH JOE!
THANKS, MA'AM. NOW, WHAT'S THE STORY WITH YOU FELLAS?
OFFICERS, IT WAS JUST A MIS-UNDERSTANDING...
UNHAPPY JOE'S RIGHT. WE'RE HERE, DISCUSS A LITTLE BUSINESS, THESE DRUNK FLYBOYS, THEY PICK A FIGHT WITH US.
THAT'S NOT TRUE. THEY WERE THREATENING HIM.
MY VOICES SAY THE LAD IS PURE, AND SPEAKS TRULY.
BUT YOU ARE OF THE DARK, AND ARE NOT CLEAN. BEST YOU BE GONE FROM HERE.
OW, £$%&...
ACH! BY MY MOTHER, THERE'S NO NEED FOR THAT! WE WERE JUST LEAVING!

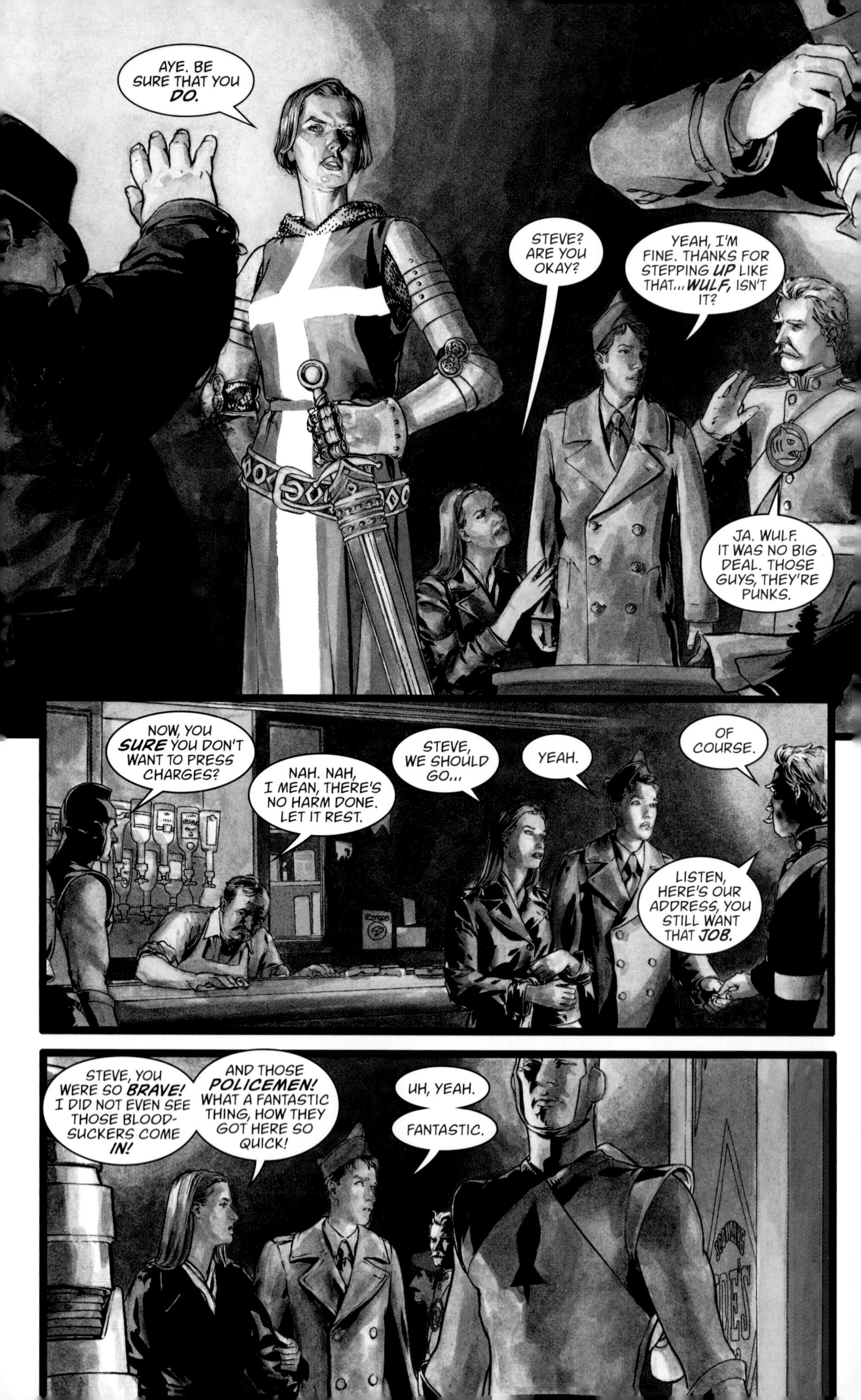
AYE. BE SURE THAT YOU DO.
STEVE? ARE YOU OKAY?
YEAH, I'M FINE. THANKS FOR STEPPING UP LIKE THAT... WULF, ISN'T IT?
JA. WULF. IT WAS NO BIG DEAL. THOSE GUYS, THEY'RE PUNKS.
NOW, YOU SURE YOU DON'T WANT TO PRESS CHARGES?
NAH. NAH, I MEAN, THERE'S NO HARM DONE. LET IT REST.
STEVE, WE SHOULD GO...
YEAH.
OF COURSE.
LISTEN, HERE'S OUR ADDRESS, YOU STILL WANT THAT JOB.
STEVE, YOU WERE SO BRAVE! I DID NOT EVEN SEE THOSE BLOOD-SUCKERS COME IN!
AND THOSE POLICEMEN! WHAT A FANTASTIC THING, HOW THEY GOT HERE SO QUICK!
UH, YEAH.
FANTASTIC.

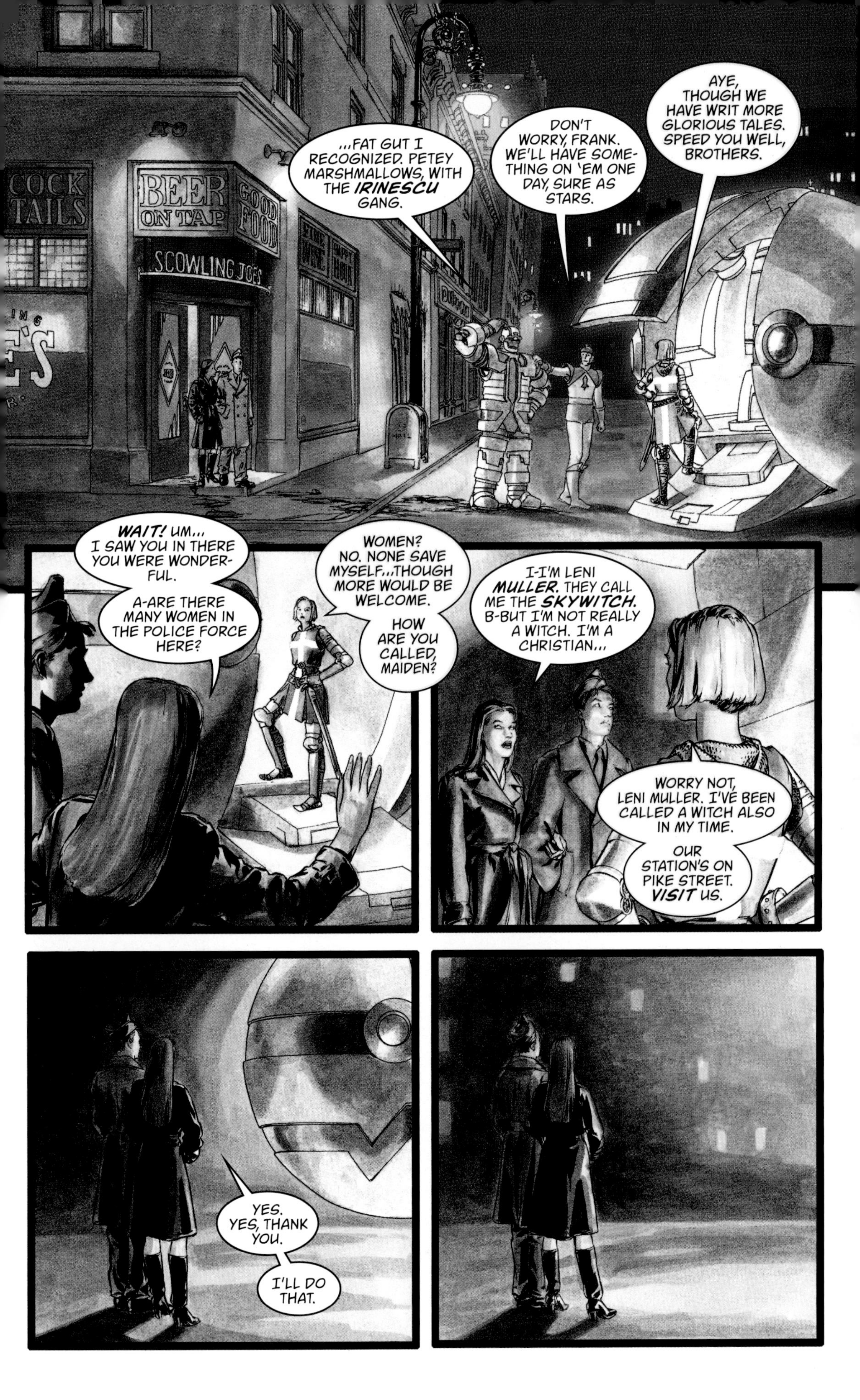
COCK TAILS
BEER ON TAP
GOOD FOOD
SCOWLING JOE'S
FINE WINE
HAPPY HOUR
...FAT GUT I RECOGNIZED. PETEY MARSHMALLOWS, WITH THE IRINESCU GANG.
DON'T WORRY, FRANK. WE'LL HAVE SOME-THING ON 'EM ONE DAY, SURE AS STARS.
AYE, THOUGH WE HAVE WRIT MORE GLORIOUS TALES. SPEED YOU WELL, BROTHERS.
WAIT! UM... I SAW YOU IN THERE YOU WERE WONDER-FUL.
A-ARE THERE MANY WOMEN IN THE POLICE FORCE HERE?
WOMEN? NO. NONE SAVE MYSELF...THOUGH MORE WOULD BE WELCOME.
HOW ARE YOU CALLED, MAIDEN?
I-I'M LENI MULLER. THEY CALL ME THE SKYWITCH. B-BUT I'M NOT REALLY A WITCH. I'M A CHRISTIAN...
WORRY NOT, LENI MULLER. I'VE BEEN CALLED A WITCH ALSO IN MY TIME.
OUR STATION'S ON PIKE STREET. VISIT US.
YES. YES, THANK YOU.
I'LL DO THAT.

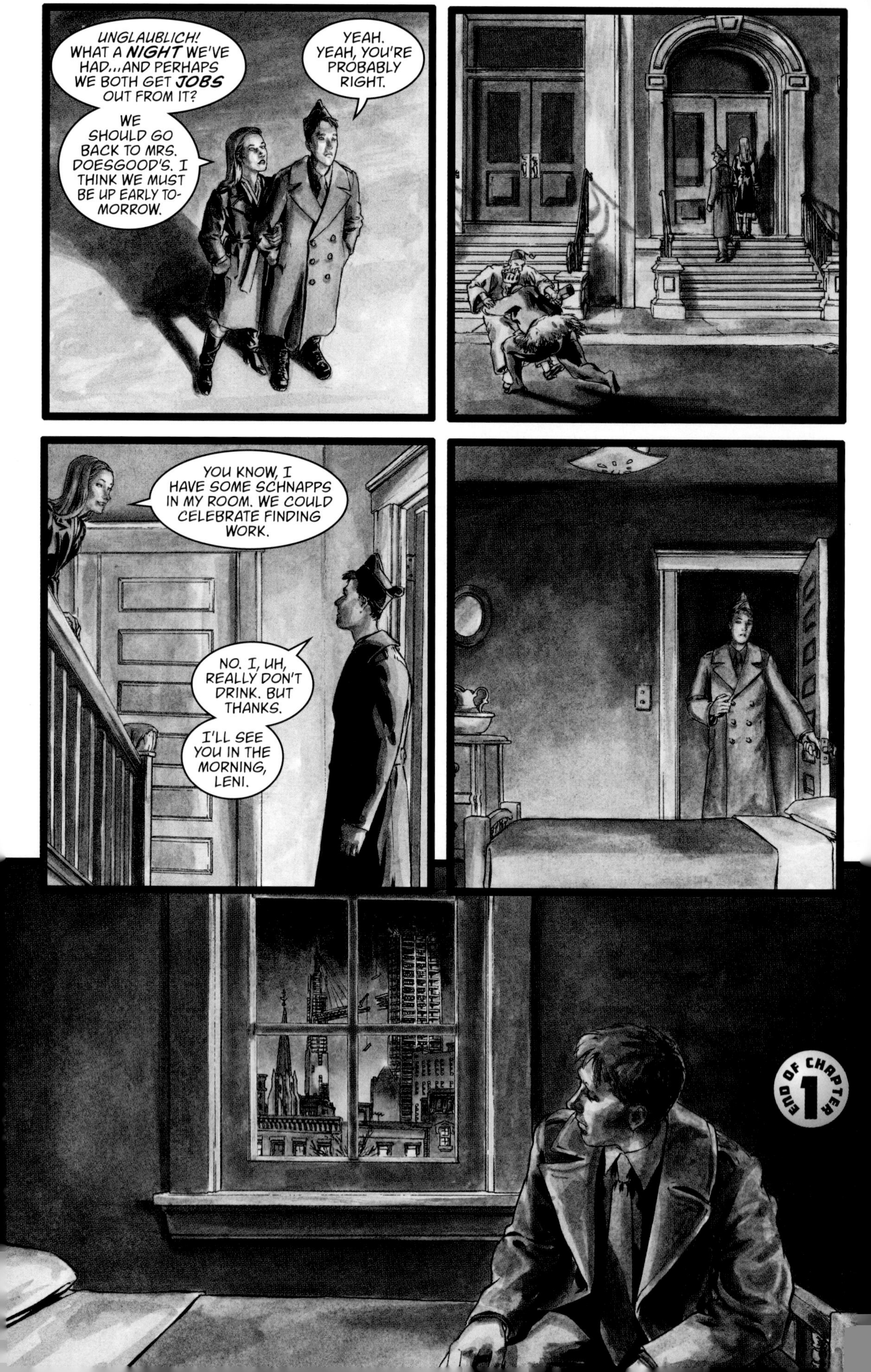
UNGLAUBLICH! WHAT A NIGHT WE'VE HAD...AND PERHAPS WE BOTH GET JOBS OUT FROM IT?
YEAH. YEAH, YOU'RE PROBABLY RIGHT.
WE SHOULD GO BACK TO MRS. DOESGOOD'S. I THINK WE MUST BE UP EARLY TO-MORROW.
YOU KNOW, I HAVE SOME SCHNAPPS IN MY ROOM. WE COULD CELEBRATE FINDING WORK.
NO. I, UH, REALLY DON'T DRINK. BUT THANKS.
I'LL SEE YOU IN THE MORNING, LENI.
END OF CHAPTER 1

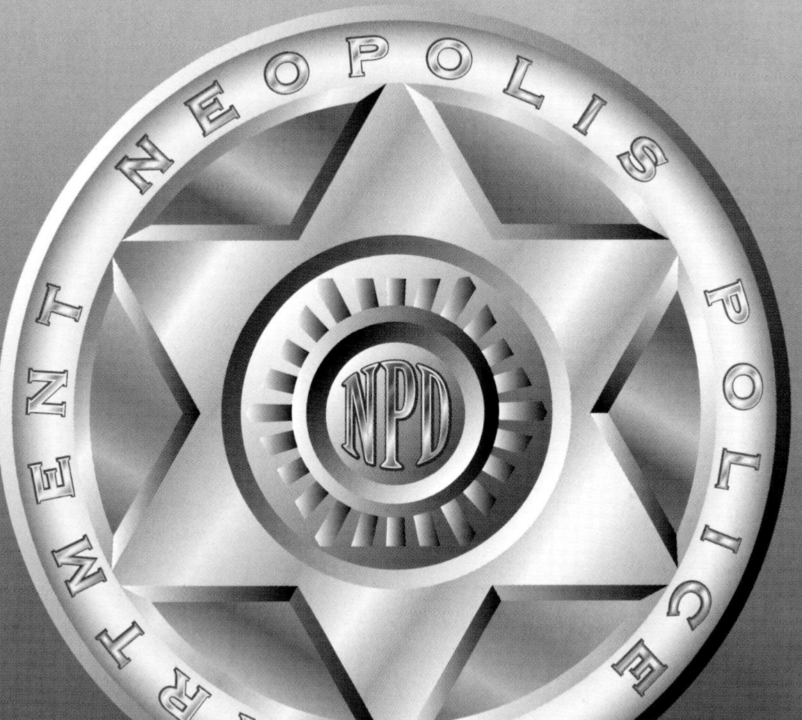
NEOPOLIS POLICE DEPARTMENT
NPD

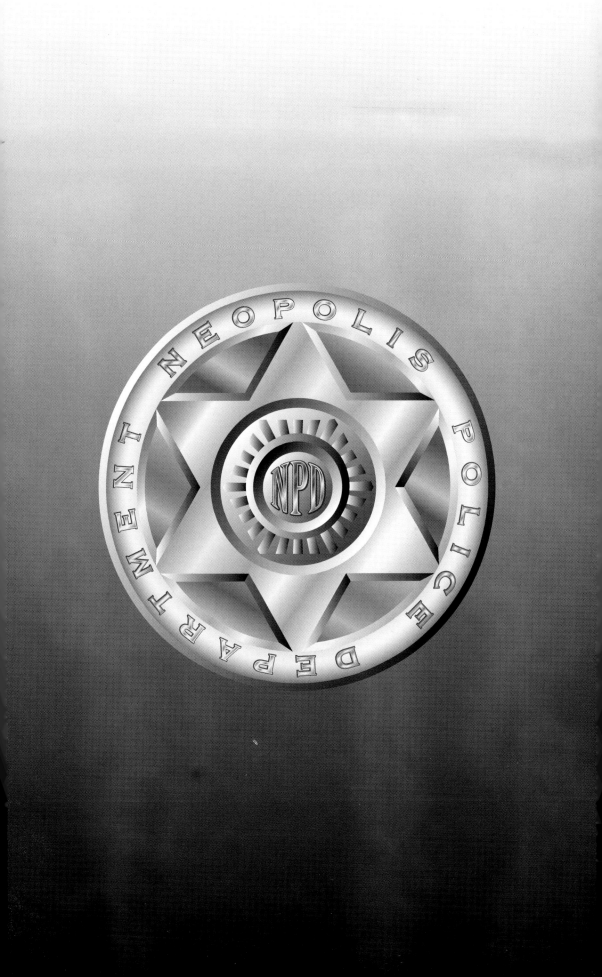

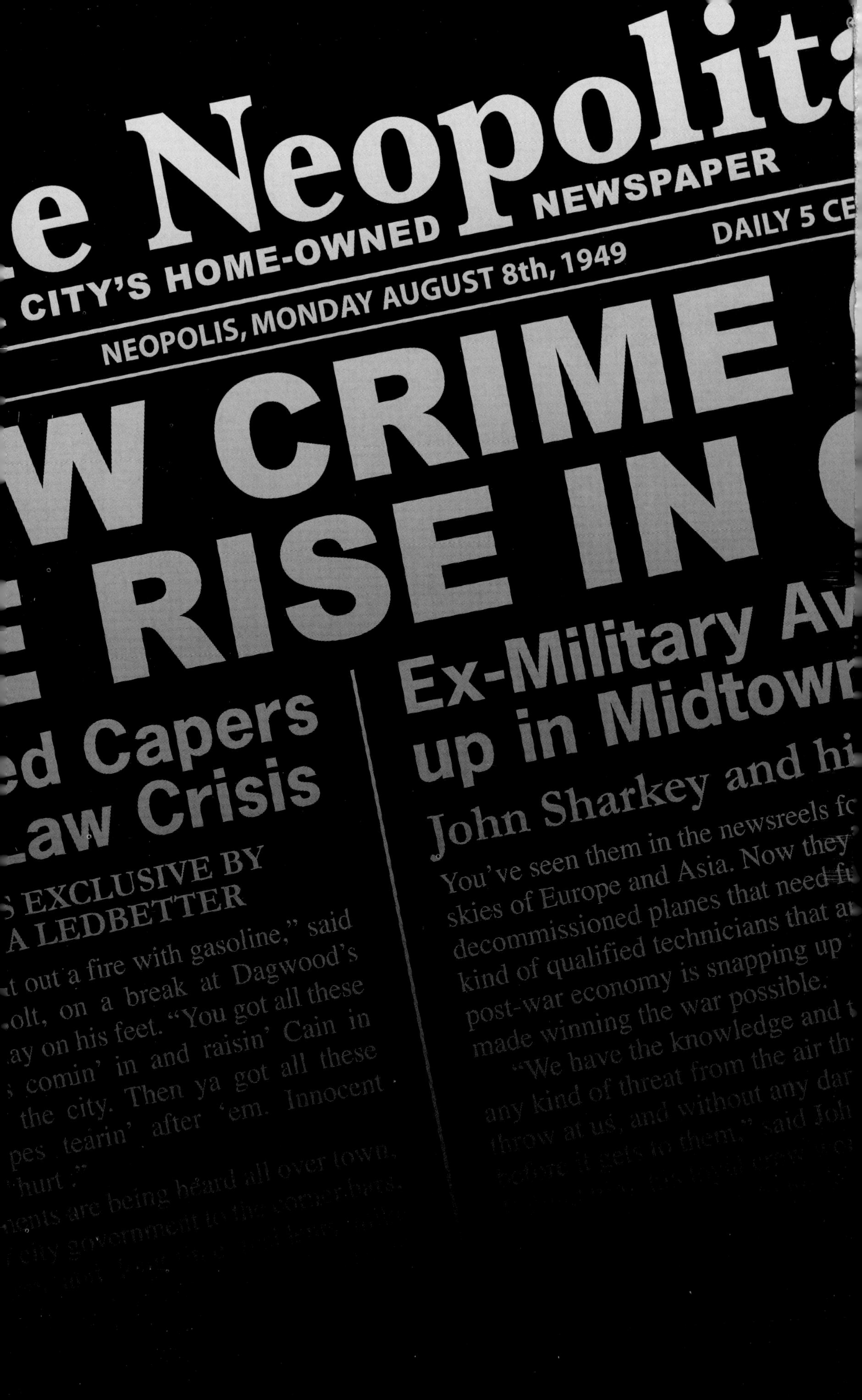

e Neopolita

CITY'S HOME-OWNED NEWSPAPER

DAILY 5 CE

NEOPOLIS, MONDAY AUGUST 8th, 1949

W CRIME
E RISE IN C

ed Capers
Law Crisis

S EXCLUSIVE BY
A LEDBETTER

t out a fire with gasoline," said
olt, on a break at Dagwood's
ay on his feet. "You got all these
s comin' in and raisin' Cain in
the city. Then ya got all these
pes tearin' after 'em. Innocent
hurt."
nents are being heard all over town,

Ex-Military Av
up in Midtown

John Sharkey and hi

You've seen them in the newsreels fo
skies of Europe and Asia. Now they'
decommissioned planes that need fu
kind of qualified technicians that ar
post-war economy is snapping up
made winning the war possible.
"We have the knowledge and t
any kind of threat from the air th
throw at us, and without any dar
before it gets to them," said Joh

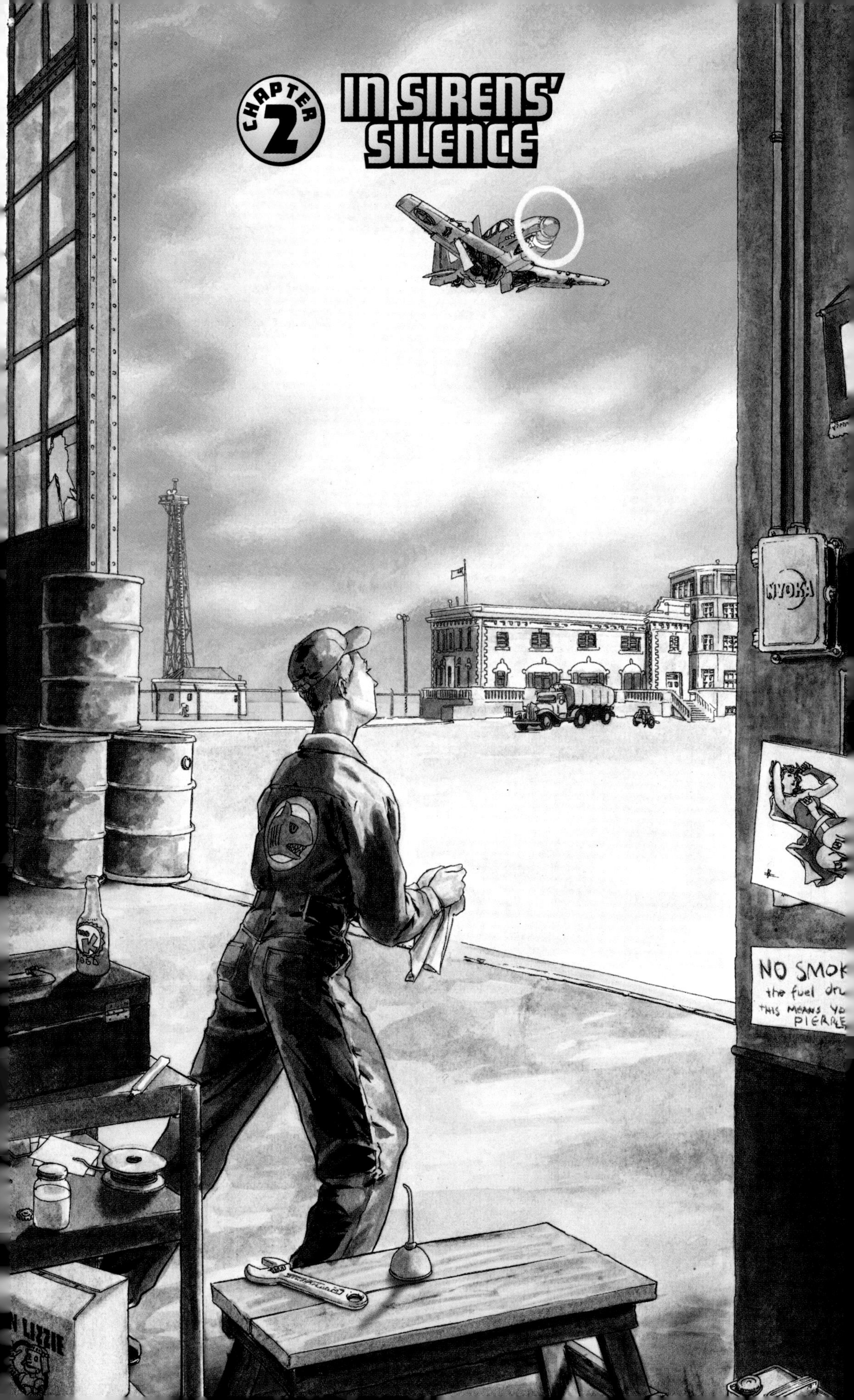
CHAPTER 2
IN SIRENS' SILENCE
NYOKA
NO SMOK
LIZZIE

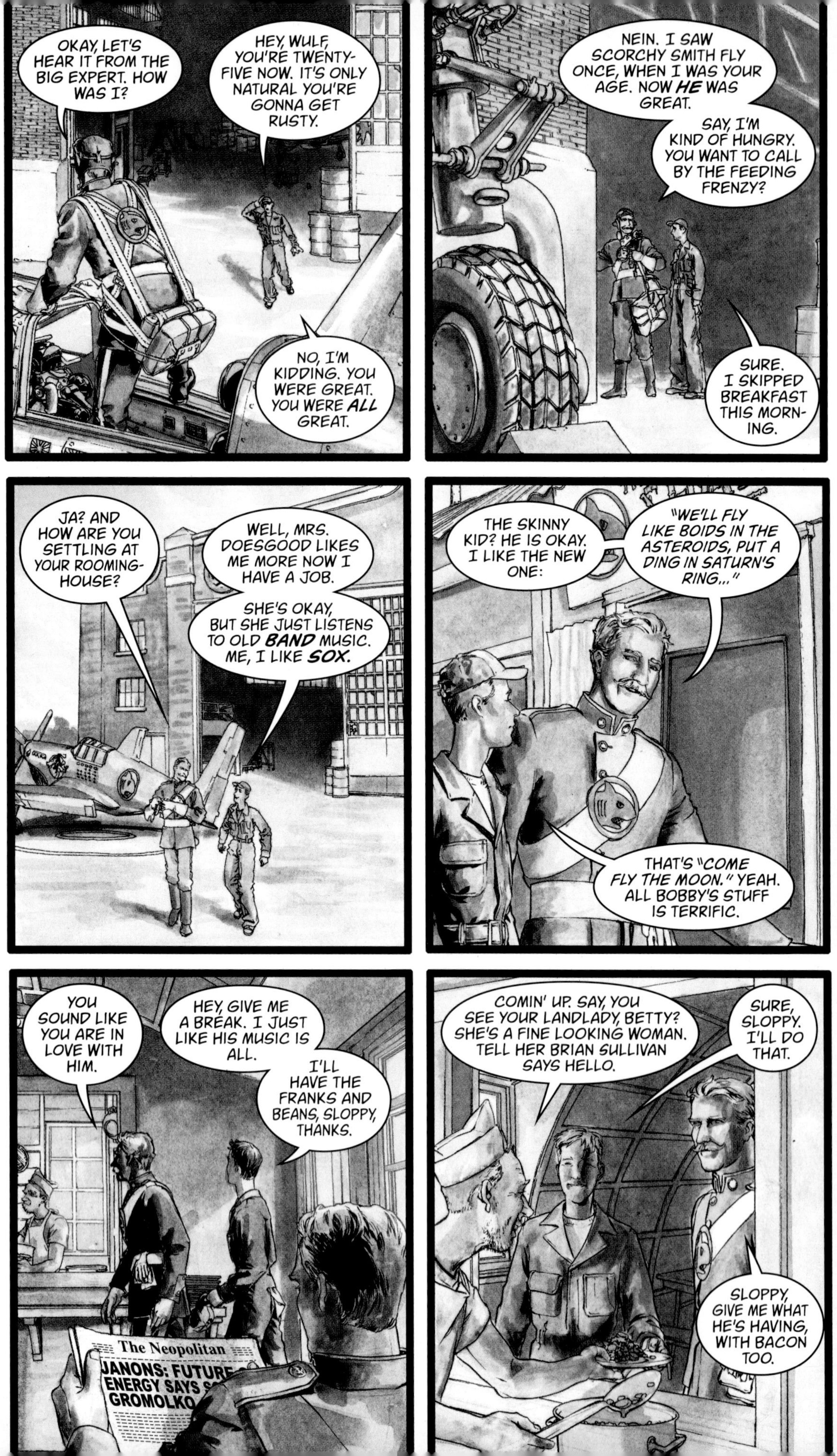
OKAY, LET'S HEAR IT FROM THE BIG EXPERT. HOW WAS I?
HEY, WULF, YOU'RE TWENTY-FIVE NOW. IT'S ONLY NATURAL YOU'RE GONNA GET RUSTY.
NO, I'M KIDDING. YOU WERE GREAT. YOU WERE ALL GREAT.
NEIN. I SAW SCORCHY SMITH FLY ONCE, WHEN I WAS YOUR AGE. NOW HE WAS GREAT.
SAY, I'M KIND OF HUNGRY. YOU WANT TO CALL BY THE FEEDING FRENZY?
SURE. I SKIPPED BREAKFAST THIS MORNING.
JA? AND HOW ARE YOU SETTLING AT YOUR ROOMING-HOUSE?
WELL, MRS. DOESGOOD LIKES ME MORE NOW I HAVE A JOB.
SHE'S OKAY, BUT SHE JUST LISTENS TO OLD BAND MUSIC. ME, I LIKE SOX.
THE SKINNY KID? HE IS OKAY. I LIKE THE NEW ONE:
"WE'LL FLY LIKE BOIDS IN THE ASTEROIDS, PUT A DING IN SATURN'S RING..."
THAT'S "COME FLY THE MOON." YEAH. ALL BOBBY'S STUFF IS TERRIFIC.
YOU SOUND LIKE YOU ARE IN LOVE WITH HIM.
HEY, GIVE ME A BREAK. I JUST LIKE HIS MUSIC IS ALL.
I'LL HAVE THE FRANKS AND BEANS, SLOPPY, THANKS.
The Neopolitan
JANONS: FUTURE ENERGY SAYS S
GROMOLKO
COMIN' UP. SAY, YOU SEE YOUR LANDLADY, BETTY? SHE'S A FINE LOOKING WOMAN. TELL HER BRIAN SULLIVAN SAYS HELLO.
SURE, SLOPPY. I'LL DO THAT.
SLOPPY, GIVE ME WHAT HE'S HAVING, WITH BACON TOO.

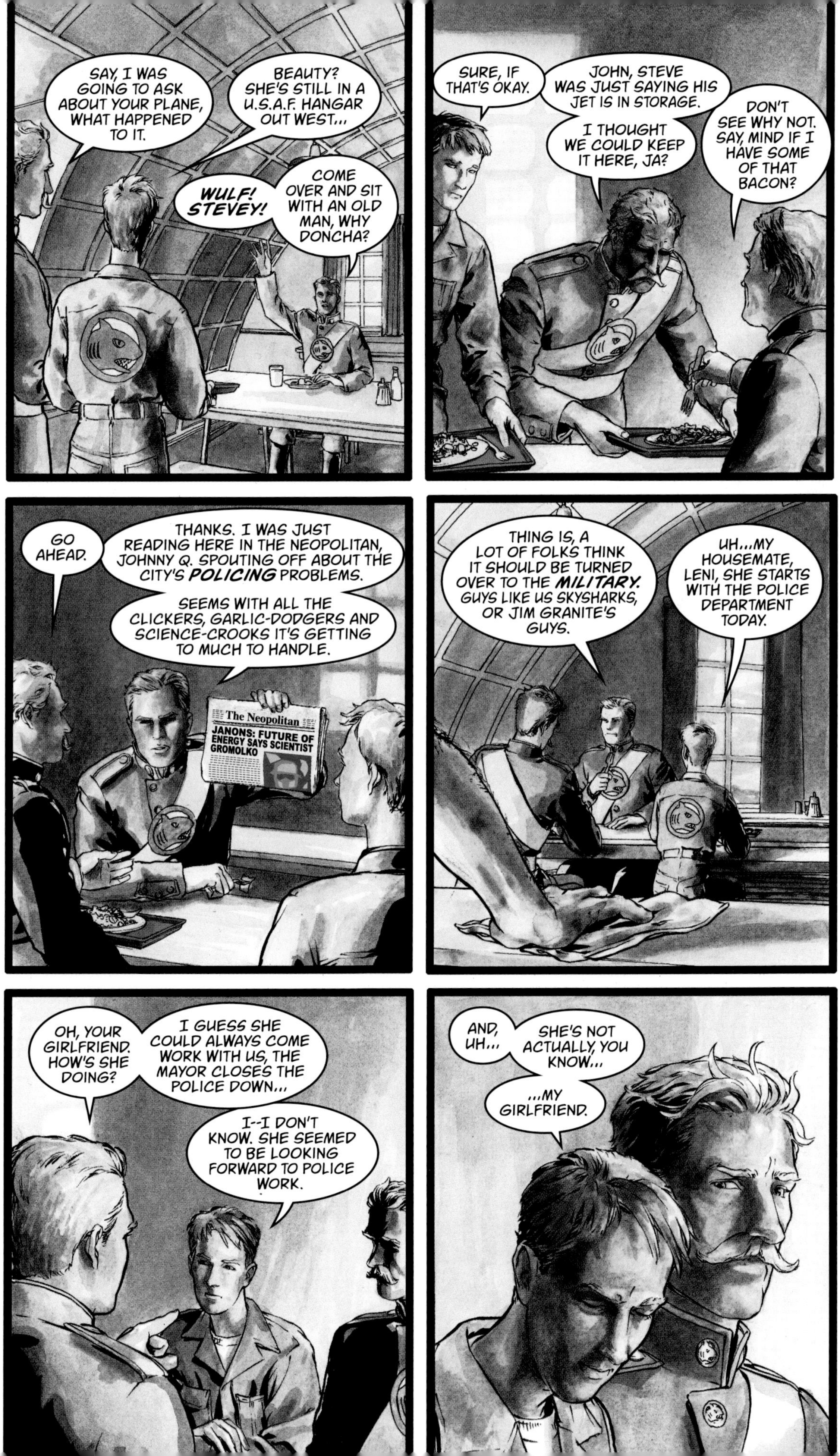
SAY, I WAS GOING TO ASK ABOUT YOUR PLANE, WHAT HAPPENED TO IT.
BEAUTY? SHE'S STILL IN A U.S.A.F. HANGAR OUT WEST...
WULF! STEVEY!
COME OVER AND SIT WITH AN OLD MAN, WHY DONCHA?
SURE, IF THAT'S OKAY.
JOHN, STEVE WAS JUST SAYING HIS JET IS IN STORAGE.
I THOUGHT WE COULD KEEP IT HERE, JA?
DON'T SEE WHY NOT. SAY, MIND IF I HAVE SOME OF THAT BACON?
GO AHEAD.
THANKS. I WAS JUST READING HERE IN THE NEOPOLITAN, JOHNNY Q. SPOUTING OFF ABOUT THE CITY'S POLICING PROBLEMS.
SEEMS WITH ALL THE CLICKERS, GARLIC-DODGERS AND SCIENCE-CROOKS IT'S GETTING TO MUCH TO HANDLE.
The Neopolitan
JANONS: FUTURE OF ENERGY SAYS SCIENTIST GROMOLKO
THING IS, A LOT OF FOLKS THINK IT SHOULD BE TURNED OVER TO THE MILITARY. GUYS LIKE US SKYSHARKS, OR JIM GRANITE'S GUYS.
UH...MY HOUSEMATE, LENI, SHE STARTS WITH THE POLICE DEPARTMENT TODAY.
OH, YOUR GIRLFRIEND. HOW'S SHE DOING?
I GUESS SHE COULD ALWAYS COME WORK WITH US, THE MAYOR CLOSES THE POLICE DOWN...
I--I DON'T KNOW. SHE SEEMED TO BE LOOKING FORWARD TO POLICE WORK.
AND, UH...
SHE'S NOT ACTUALLY, YOU KNOW...
...MY GIRLFRIEND.

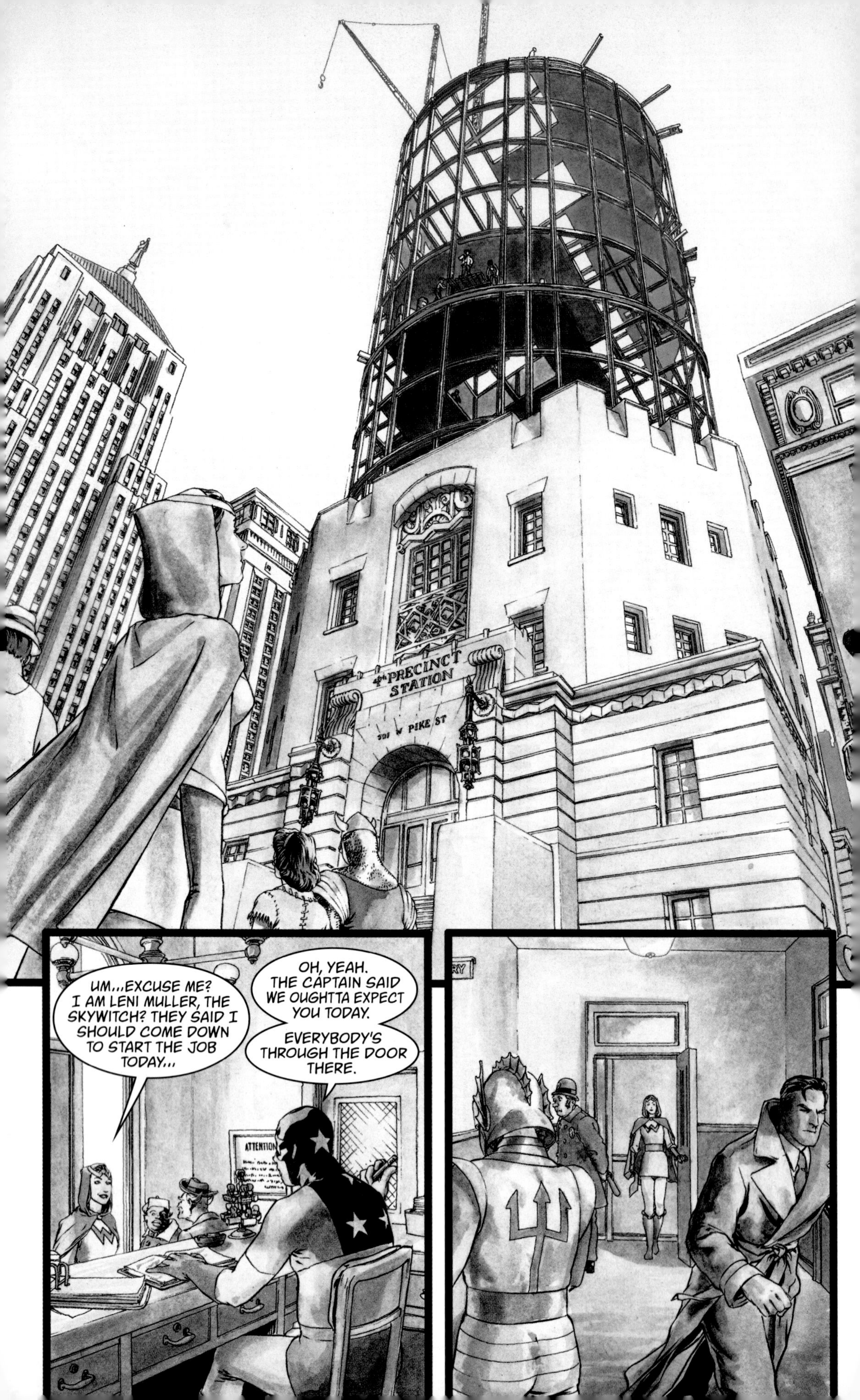
4th PRECINCT STATION
501 W PIKE ST
UM...EXCUSE ME? I AM LENI MULLER, THE SKYWITCH? THEY SAID I SHOULD COME DOWN TO START THE JOB TODAY...
OH, YEAH. THE CAPTAIN SAID WE OUGHTTA EXPECT YOU TODAY.
EVERYBODY'S THROUGH THE DOOR THERE.
ATTENTION

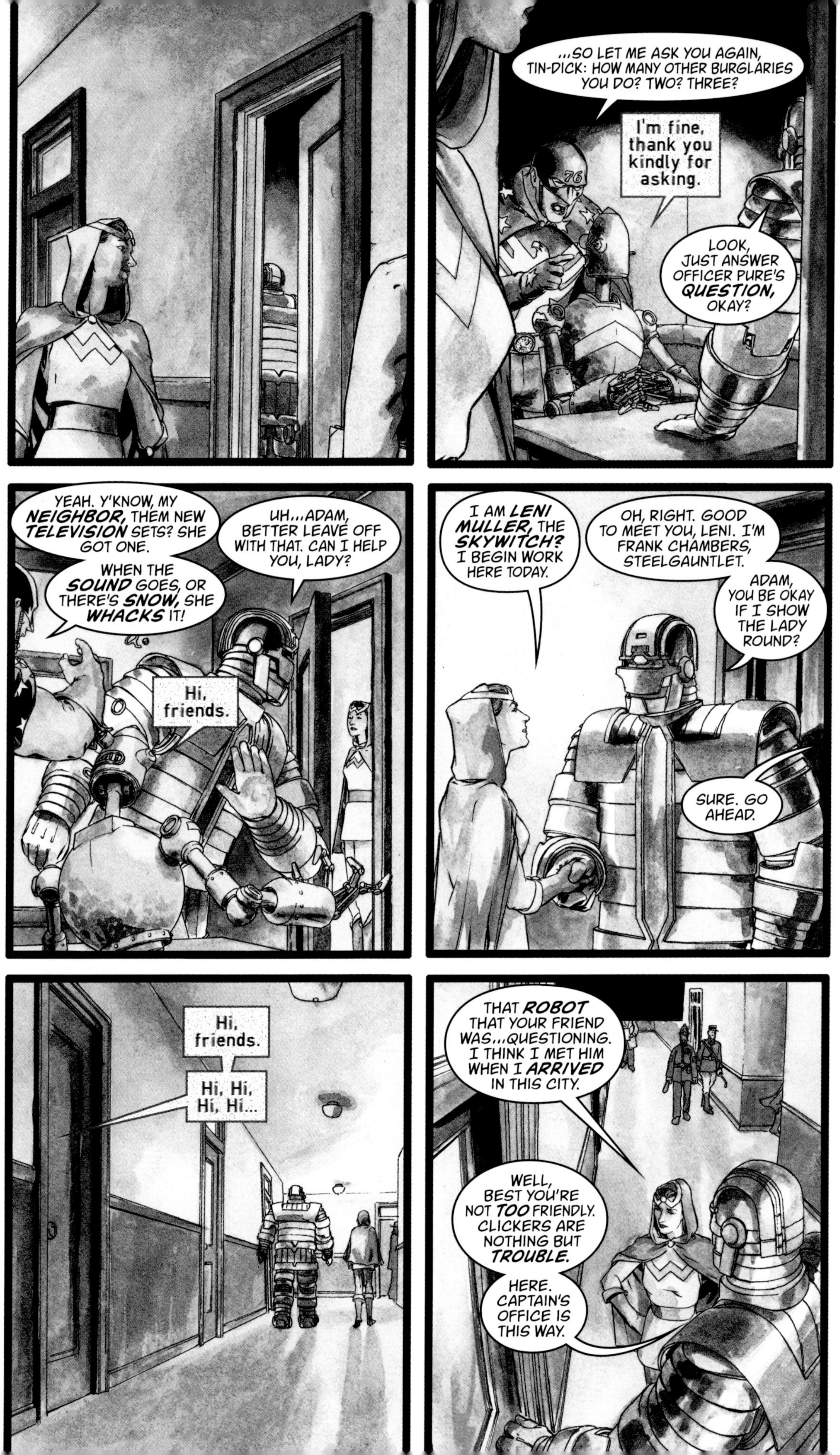
...SO LET ME ASK YOU AGAIN, TIN-DICK: HOW MANY OTHER BURGLARIES YOU DO? TWO? THREE?
I'm fine, thank you kindly for asking.
LOOK, JUST ANSWER OFFICER PURE'S QUESTION, OKAY?
YEAH. Y'KNOW, MY NEIGHBOR, THEM NEW TELEVISION SETS? SHE GOT ONE.
WHEN THE SOUND GOES, OR THERE'S SNOW, SHE WHACKS IT!
UH...ADAM, BETTER LEAVE OFF WITH THAT. CAN I HELP YOU, LADY?
Hi, friends.
I AM LENI MULLER, THE SKYWITCH? I BEGIN WORK HERE TODAY.
OH, RIGHT. GOOD TO MEET YOU, LENI. I'M FRANK CHAMBERS, STEELGAUNTLET.
ADAM, YOU BE OKAY IF I SHOW THE LADY ROUND?
SURE. GO AHEAD.
Hi, friends.
Hi, Hi, Hi, Hi...
THAT ROBOT THAT YOUR FRIEND WAS...QUESTIONING. I THINK I MET HIM WHEN I ARRIVED IN THIS CITY.
WELL, BEST YOU'RE NOT TOO FRIENDLY. CLICKERS ARE NOTHING BUT TROUBLE.
HERE. CAPTAIN'S OFFICE IS THIS WAY.

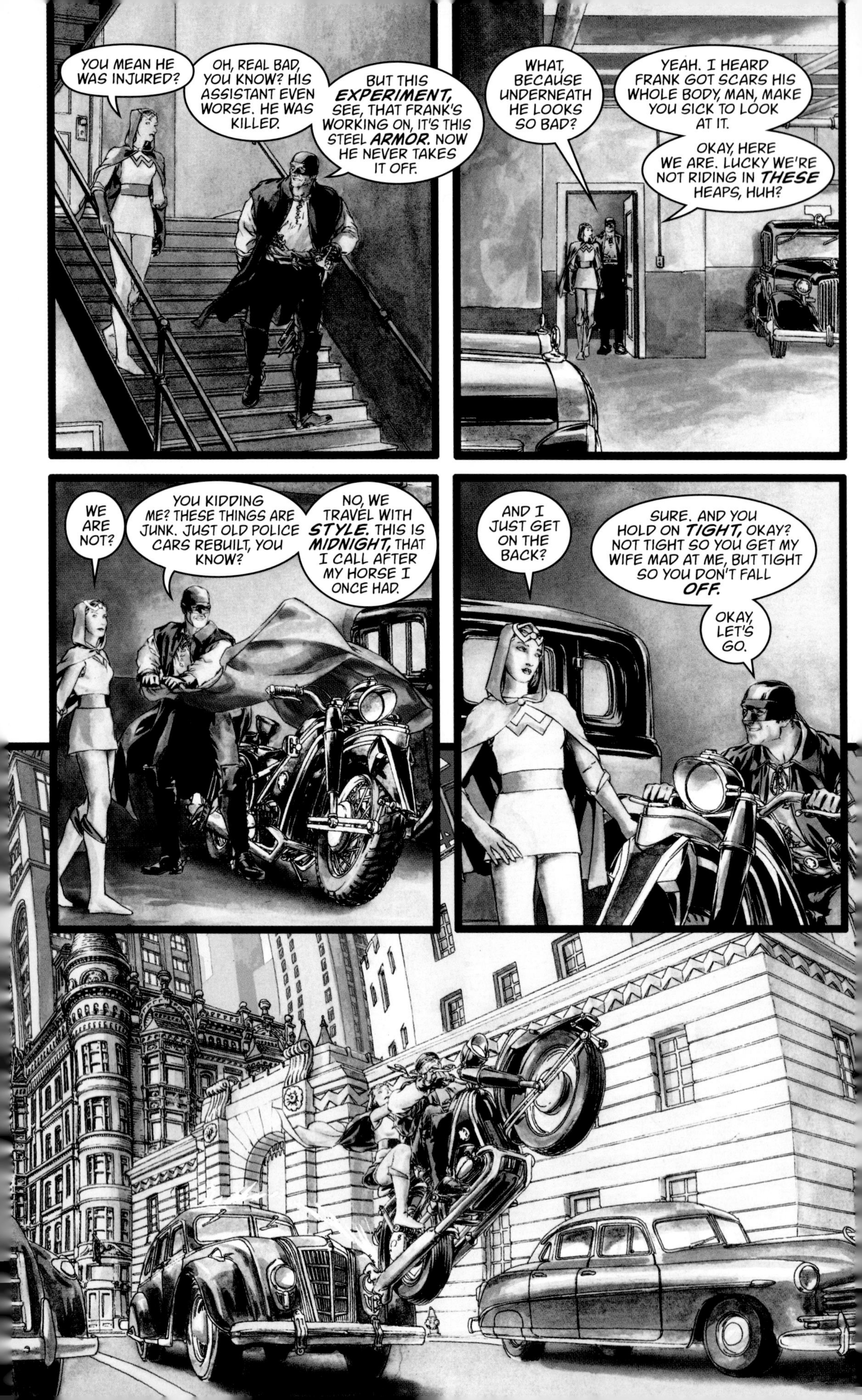
YOU MEAN HE WAS INJURED?
OH, REAL BAD, YOU KNOW? HIS ASSISTANT EVEN WORSE. HE WAS KILLED.
BUT THIS *EXPERIMENT,* SEE, THAT FRANK'S WORKING ON, IT'S THIS STEEL *ARMOR.* NOW HE NEVER TAKES IT OFF.
WHAT, BECAUSE UNDERNEATH HE LOOKS SO BAD?
YEAH. I HEARD FRANK GOT SCARS HIS WHOLE BODY, MAN, MAKE YOU SICK TO LOOK AT IT.
OKAY, HERE WE ARE. LUCKY WE'RE NOT RIDING IN *THESE* HEAPS, HUH?
WE ARE NOT?
YOU KIDDING ME? THESE THINGS ARE JUNK. JUST OLD POLICE CARS REBUILT, YOU KNOW?
NO, WE TRAVEL WITH *STYLE.* THIS IS *MIDNIGHT,* THAT I CALL AFTER MY HORSE I ONCE HAD.
AND I JUST GET ON THE BACK?
SURE. AND YOU HOLD ON *TIGHT,* OKAY? NOT TIGHT SO YOU GET MY WIFE MAD AT ME, BUT TIGHT SO YOU DON'T FALL *OFF.*
OKAY, LET'S GO.

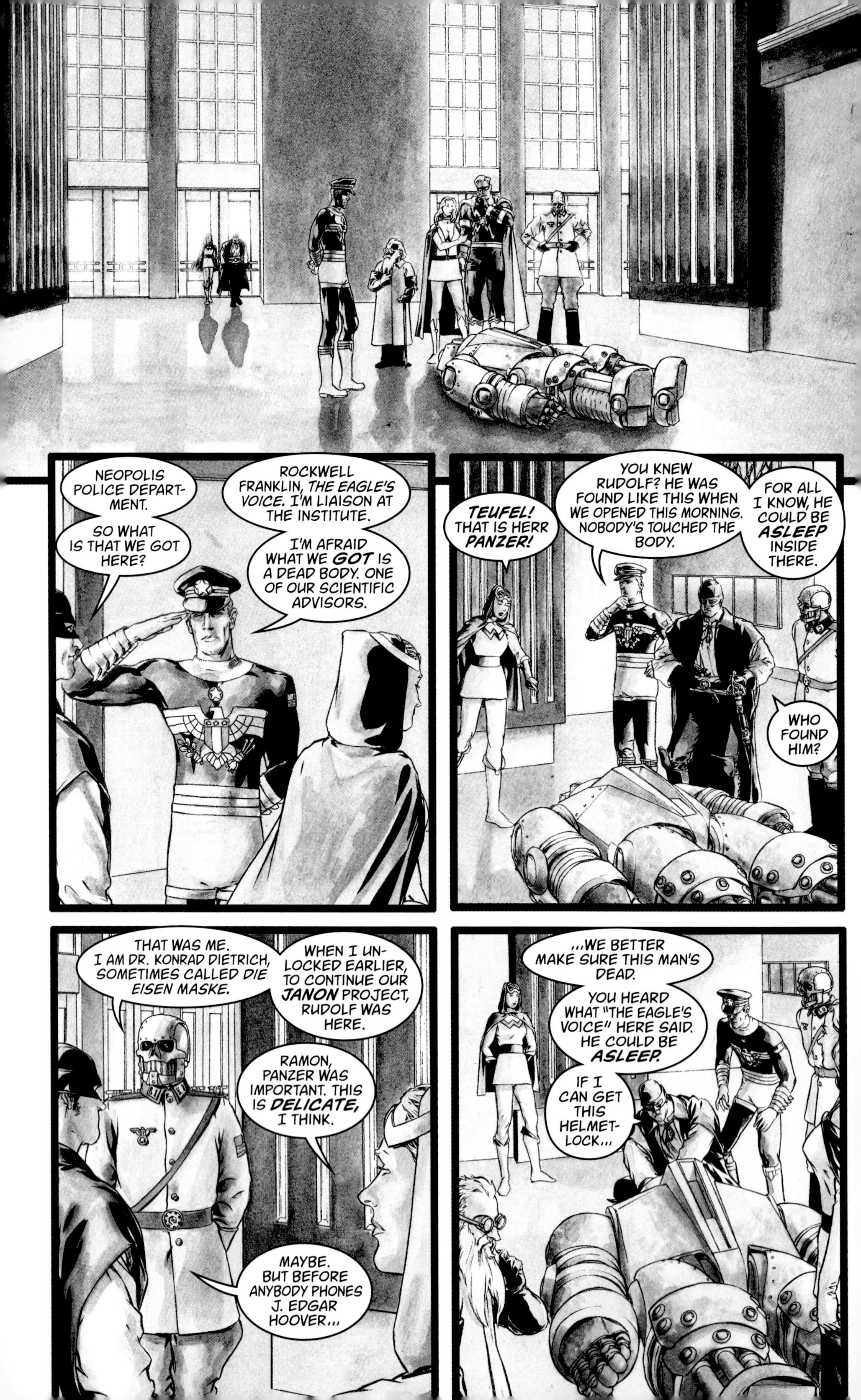
NEOPOLIS POLICE DEPARTMENT.
SO WHAT IS THAT WE GOT HERE?
ROCKWELL FRANKLIN, THE EAGLE'S VOICE. I'M LIAISON AT THE INSTITUTE.
I'M AFRAID WHAT WE GOT IS A DEAD BODY. ONE OF OUR SCIENTIFIC ADVISORS.
TEUFEL! THAT IS HERR PANZER!
YOU KNEW RUDOLF? HE WAS FOUND LIKE THIS WHEN WE OPENED THIS MORNING. NOBODY'S TOUCHED THE BODY.
FOR ALL I KNOW, HE COULD BE ASLEEP INSIDE THERE.
WHO FOUND HIM?
THAT WAS ME. I AM DR. KONRAD DIETRICH, SOMETIMES CALLED DIE EISEN MASKE.
WHEN I UNLOCKED EARLIER, TO CONTINUE OUR JANON PROJECT, RUDOLF WAS HERE.
RAMON, PANZER WAS IMPORTANT. THIS IS DELICATE, I THINK.
MAYBE. BUT BEFORE ANYBODY PHONES J. EDGAR HOOVER...
...WE BETTER MAKE SURE THIS MAN'S DEAD.
YOU HEARD WHAT "THE EAGLE'S VOICE" HERE SAID. HE COULD BE ASLEEP.
IF I CAN GET THIS HELMET-LOCK...

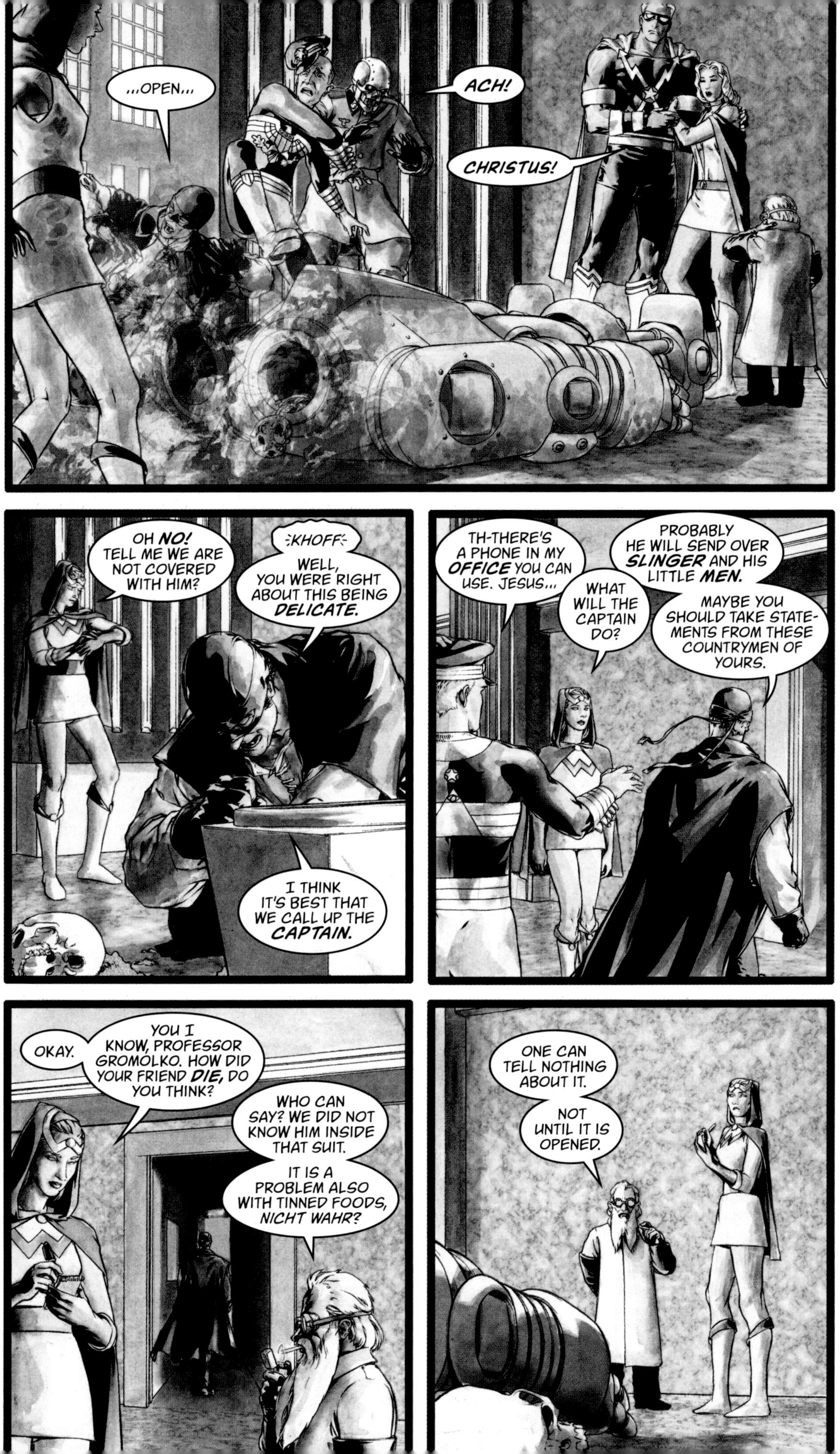
...OPEN...
ACH!
CHRISTUS!
OH NO! TELL ME WE ARE NOT COVERED WITH HIM?
KHOFF
WELL, YOU WERE RIGHT ABOUT THIS BEING DELICATE.
I THINK IT'S BEST THAT WE CALL UP THE CAPTAIN.
TH-THERE'S A PHONE IN MY OFFICE YOU CAN USE. JESUS...
WHAT WILL THE CAPTAIN DO?
PROBABLY HE WILL SEND OVER SLINGER AND HIS LITTLE MEN.
MAYBE YOU SHOULD TAKE STATE-MENTS FROM THESE COUNTRYMEN OF YOURS.
OKAY.
YOU I KNOW, PROFESSOR GROMOLKO. HOW DID YOUR FRIEND DIE, DO YOU THINK?
WHO CAN SAY? WE DID NOT KNOW HIM INSIDE THAT SUIT.
IT IS A PROBLEM ALSO WITH TINNED FOODS, NICHT WAHR?
ONE CAN TELL NOTHING ABOUT IT.
NOT UNTIL IT IS OPENED.

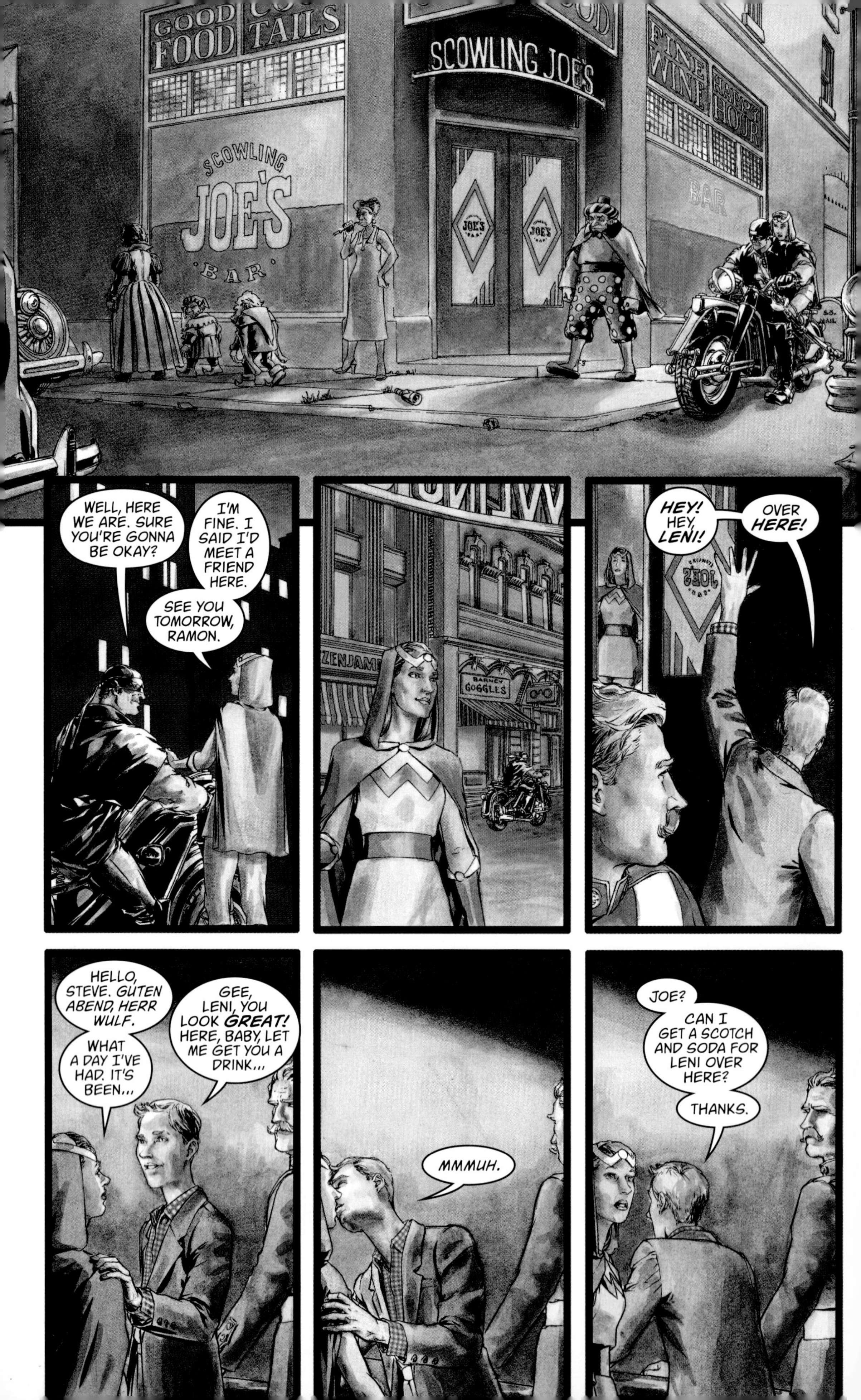
GOOD FOOD
TAILS
SCOWLING JOE'S
FINE WINE
HAPPY HOUR
SCOWLING JOE'S BAR
BAR
WELL, HERE WE ARE. SURE YOU'RE GONNA BE OKAY?
I'M FINE. I SAID I'D MEET A FRIEND HERE.
SEE YOU TOMORROW, RAMON.
BARNEY GOGGLES
HEY! HEY, LENI!
OVER HERE!
HELLO, STEVE. GUTEN ABEND, HERR WULF.
WHAT A DAY I'VE HAD. IT'S BEEN...
GEE, LENI, YOU LOOK GREAT! HERE, BABY, LET ME GET YOU A DRINK...
MMMUH.
JOE?
CAN I GET A SCOTCH AND SODA FOR LENI OVER HERE?
THANKS.

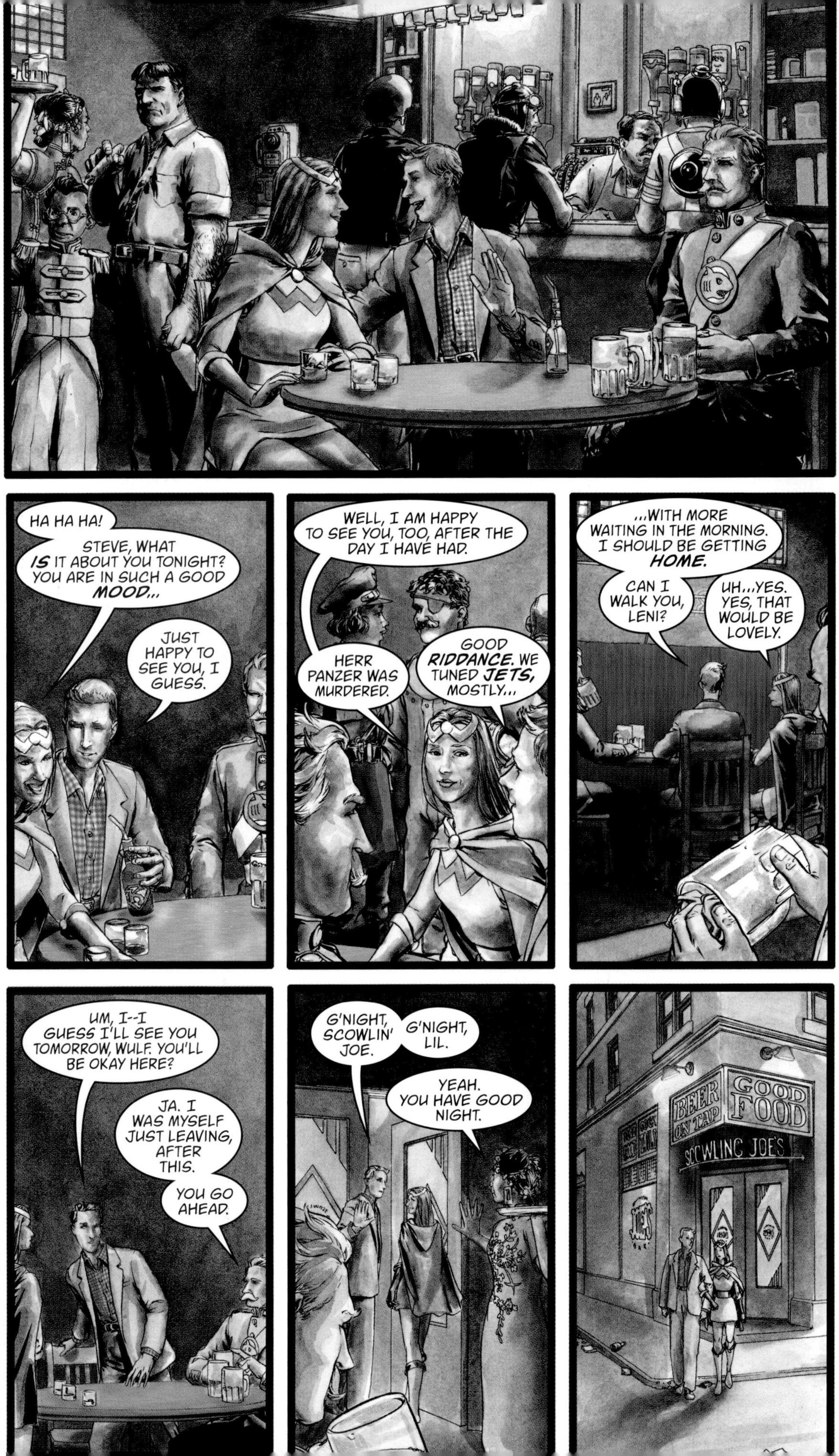
HA HA HA!
STEVE, WHAT IS IT ABOUT YOU TONIGHT? YOU ARE IN SUCH A GOOD MOOD...
JUST HAPPY TO SEE YOU, I GUESS.
WELL, I AM HAPPY TO SEE YOU, TOO, AFTER THE DAY I HAVE HAD.
HERR PANZER WAS MURDERED.
GOOD RIDDANCE. WE TUNED JETS, MOSTLY...
...WITH MORE WAITING IN THE MORNING. I SHOULD BE GETTING HOME.
CAN I WALK YOU, LENI?
UH...YES. YES, THAT WOULD BE LOVELY.
UM, I--I GUESS I'LL SEE YOU TOMORROW, WULF. YOU'LL BE OKAY HERE?
JA. I WAS MYSELF JUST LEAVING, AFTER THIS.
YOU GO AHEAD.
G'NIGHT, SCOWLIN' JOE.
G'NIGHT, LIL.
YEAH. YOU HAVE GOOD NIGHT.
BEER ON TAP
GOOD FOOD
SCOWLING JOE'S

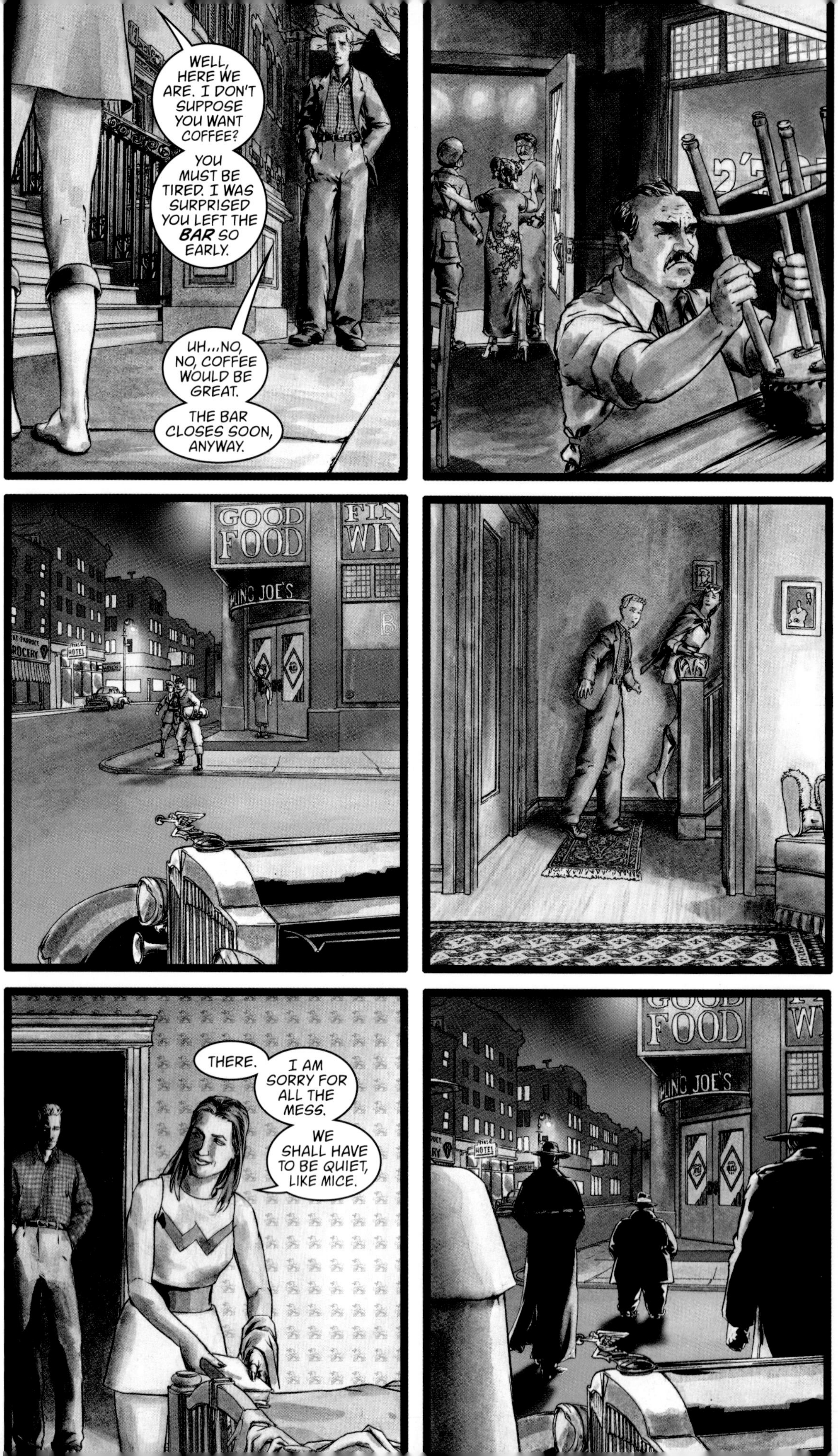

WELL, HERE WE ARE. I DON'T SUPPOSE YOU WANT COFFEE?
YOU MUST BE TIRED. I WAS SURPRISED YOU LEFT THE **BAR** SO EARLY.
UH...NO, NO, COFFEE WOULD BE GREAT.
THE BAR CLOSES SOON, ANYWAY.
GOOD FOOD
HOTEL
THERE.
I AM SORRY FOR ALL THE MESS.
WE SHALL HAVE TO BE QUIET, LIKE MICE.
GOOD FOOD
HOTEL

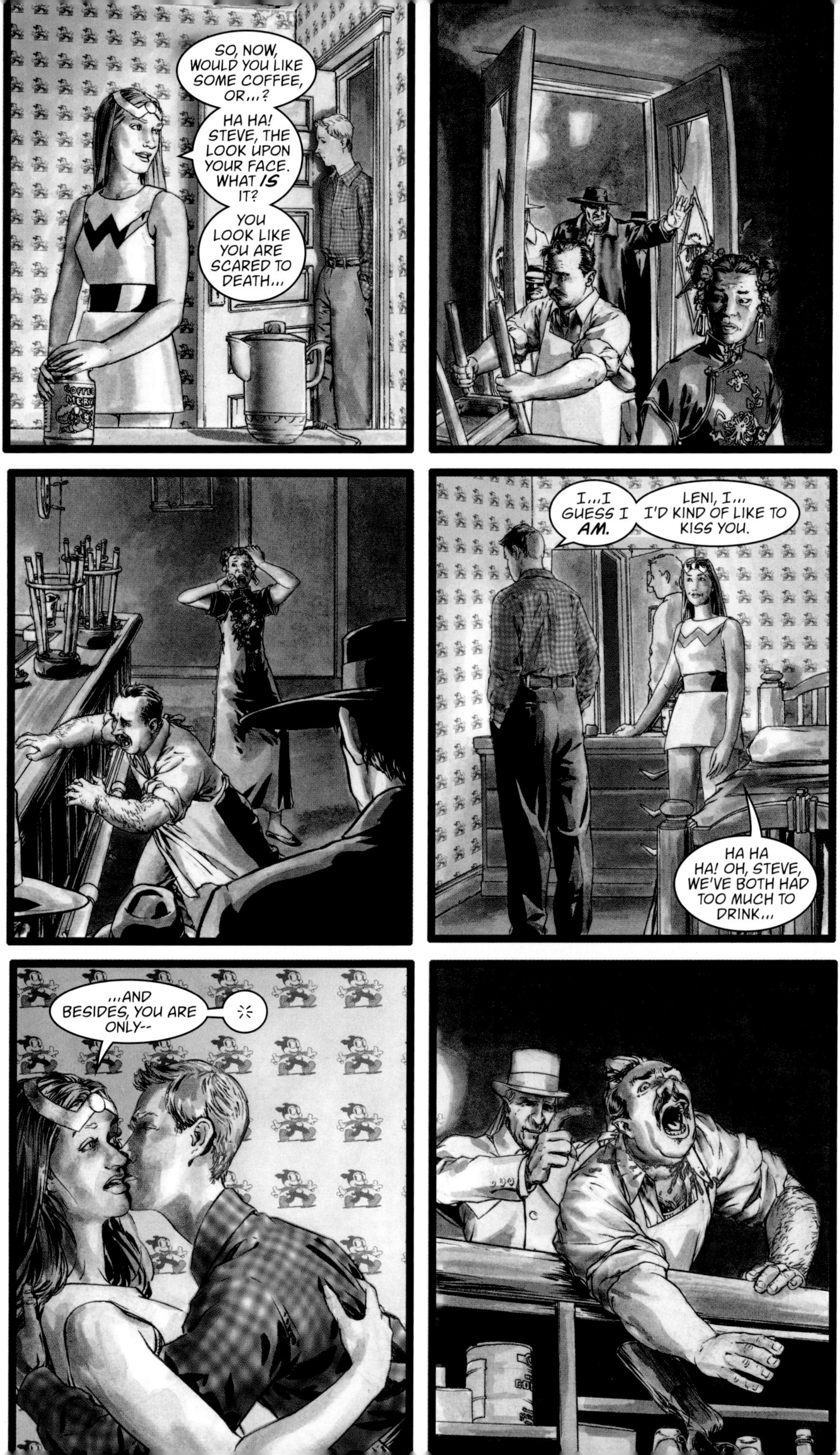
SO, NOW, WOULD YOU LIKE SOME COFFEE, OR...?
HA HA! STEVE, THE LOOK UPON YOUR FACE. WHAT *IS* IT?
YOU LOOK LIKE YOU ARE SCARED TO DEATH...
I...I GUESS I **AM.**
LENI, I... I'D KIND OF LIKE TO KISS YOU.
HA HA HA! OH, STEVE, WE'VE BOTH HAD TOO MUCH TO DRINK...
...AND BESIDES, YOU ARE ONLY--

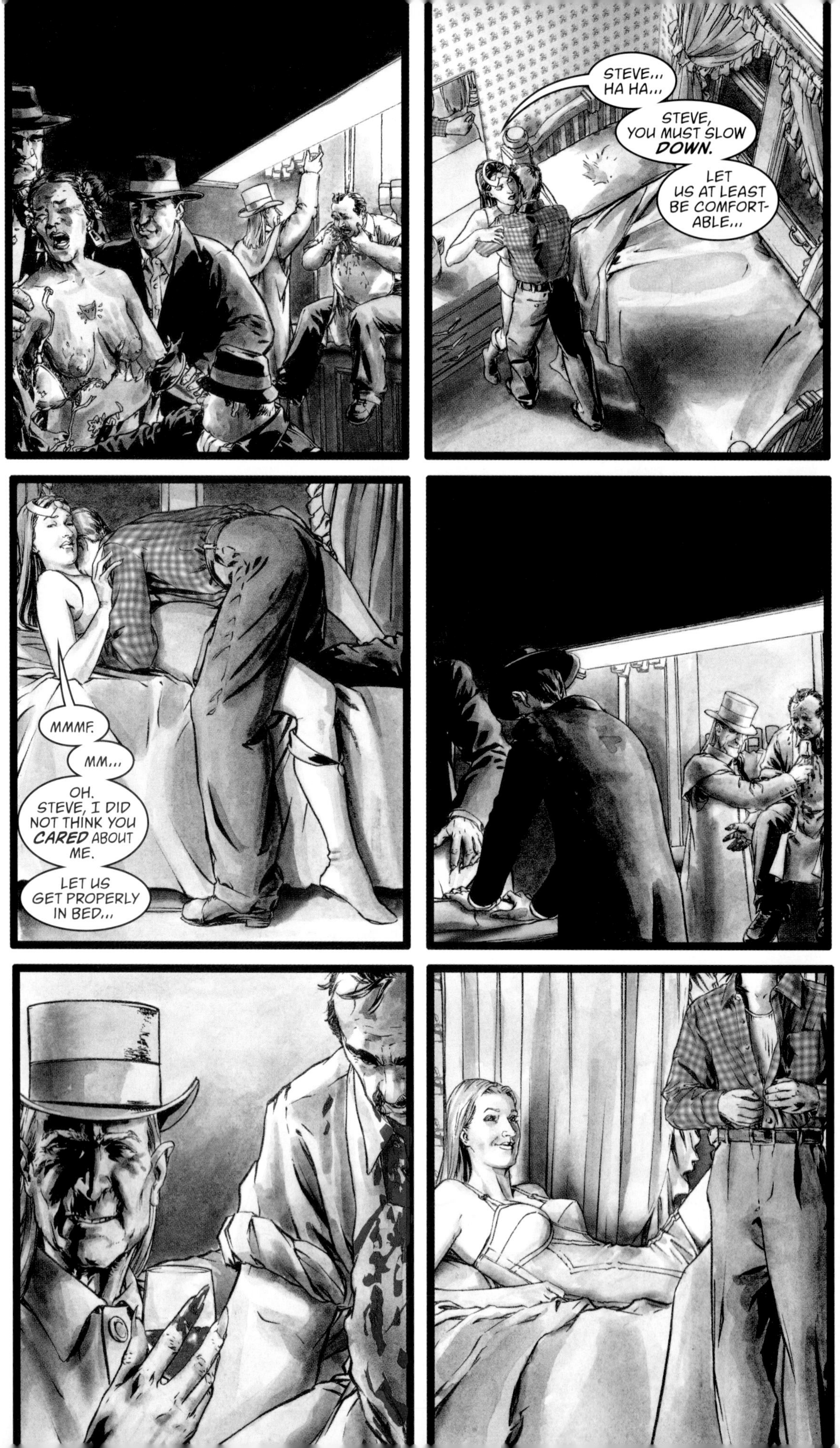
STEVE... HA HA...
STEVE, YOU MUST SLOW DOWN.
LET US AT LEAST BE COMFORT-ABLE...
MMMF.
MM...
OH. STEVE, I DID NOT THINK YOU CARED ABOUT ME.
LET US GET PROPERLY IN BED...

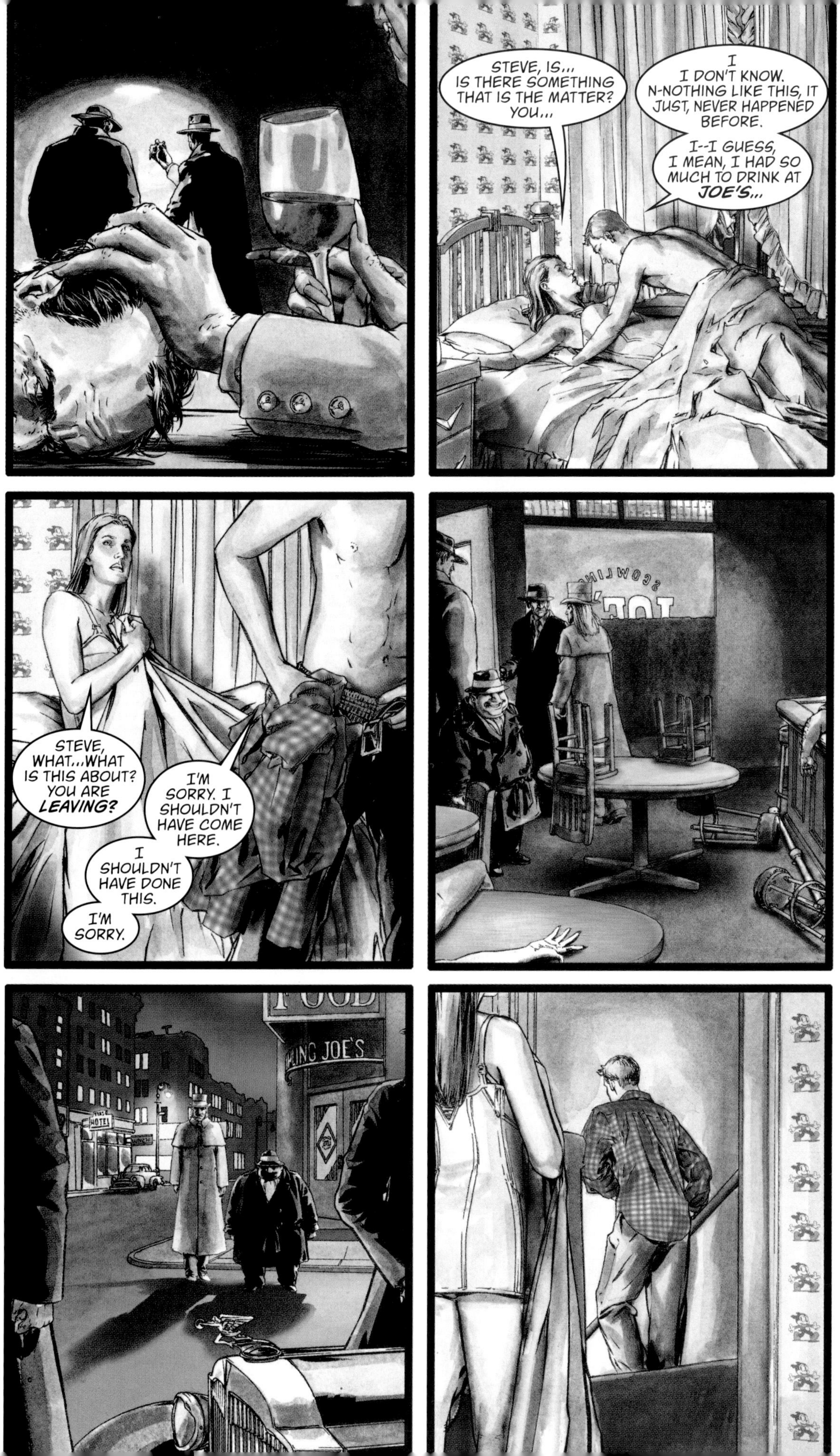
STEVE, IS... IS THERE SOMETHING THAT IS THE MATTER? YOU...
I I DON'T KNOW. N-NOTHING LIKE THIS, IT JUST, NEVER HAPPENED BEFORE.
I--I GUESS, I MEAN, I HAD SO MUCH TO DRINK AT JOE'S...
STEVE, WHAT...WHAT IS THIS ABOUT? YOU ARE LEAVING?
I'M SORRY. I SHOULDN'T HAVE COME HERE.
I SHOULDN'T HAVE DONE THIS.
I'M SORRY.
FOOD
LING JOE'S
HOTEL

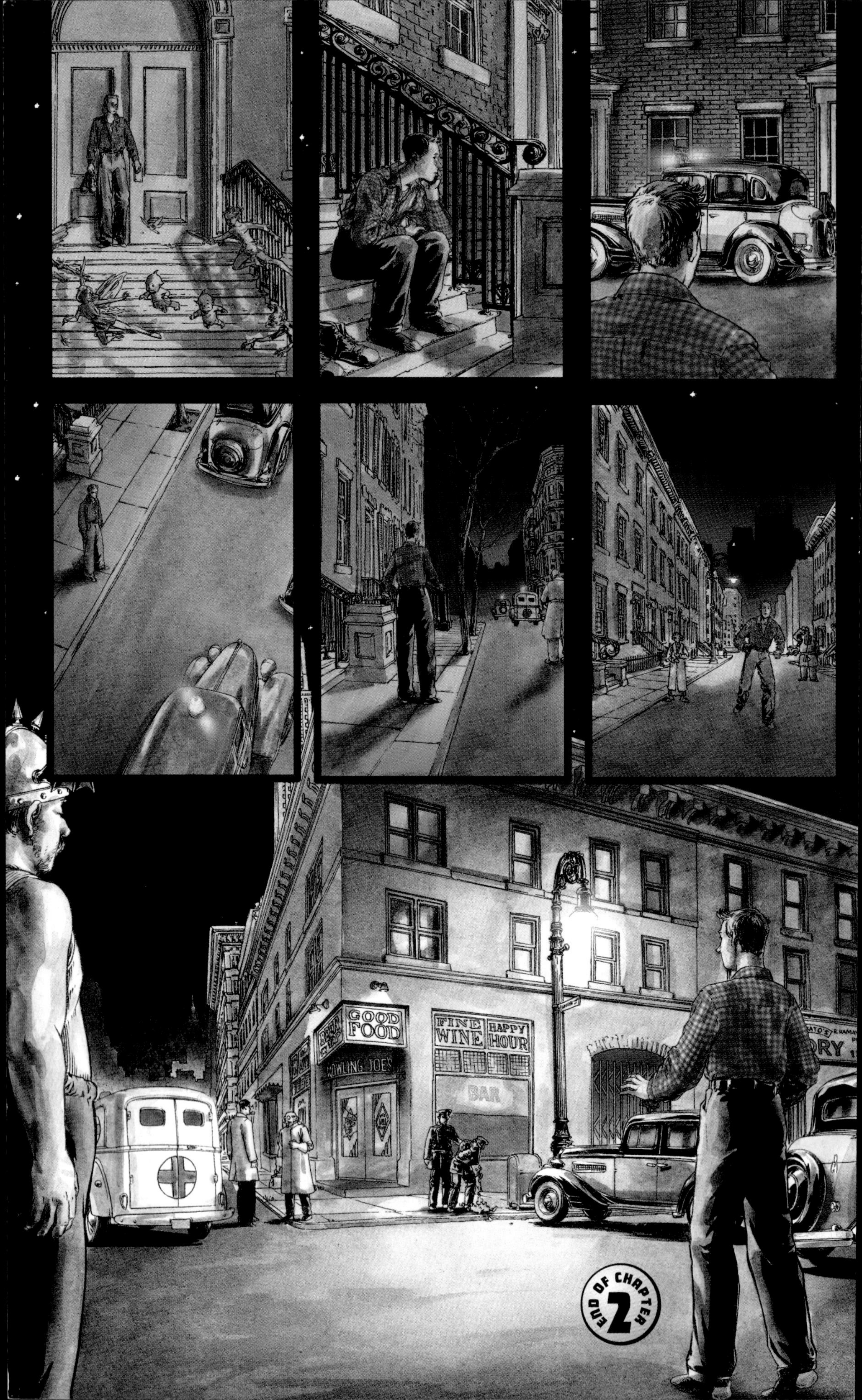
GOOD FOOD
FINE WINE
HAPPY HOUR
HOWLING JOE'S
BAR
END OF CHAPTER 2

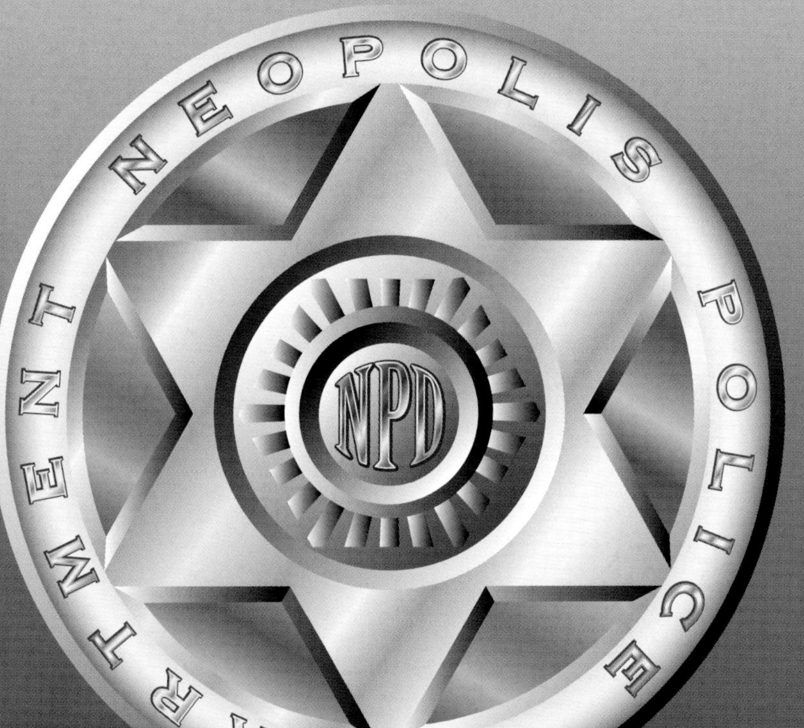
NEOPOLIS POLICE DEPARTMENT
NPD

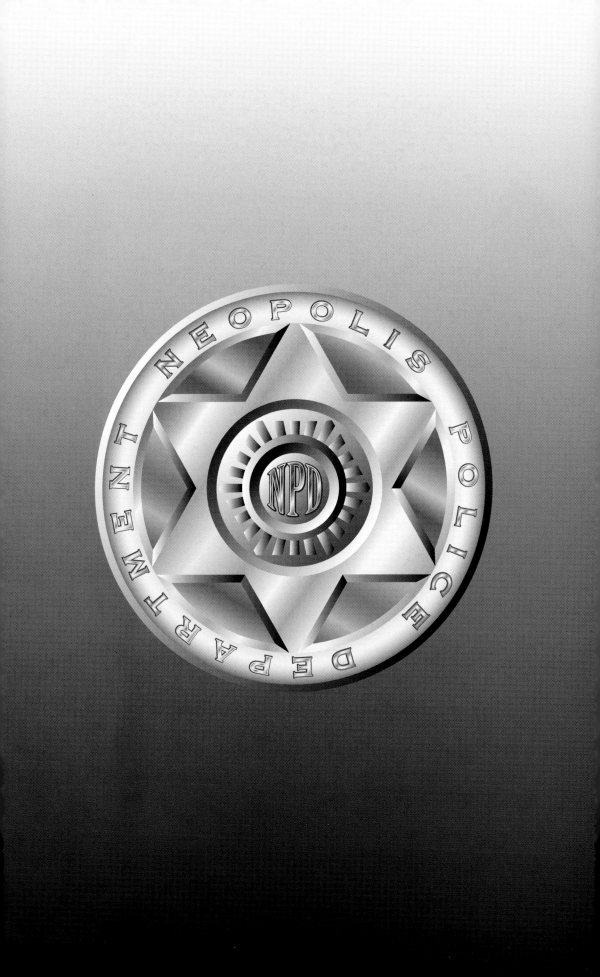

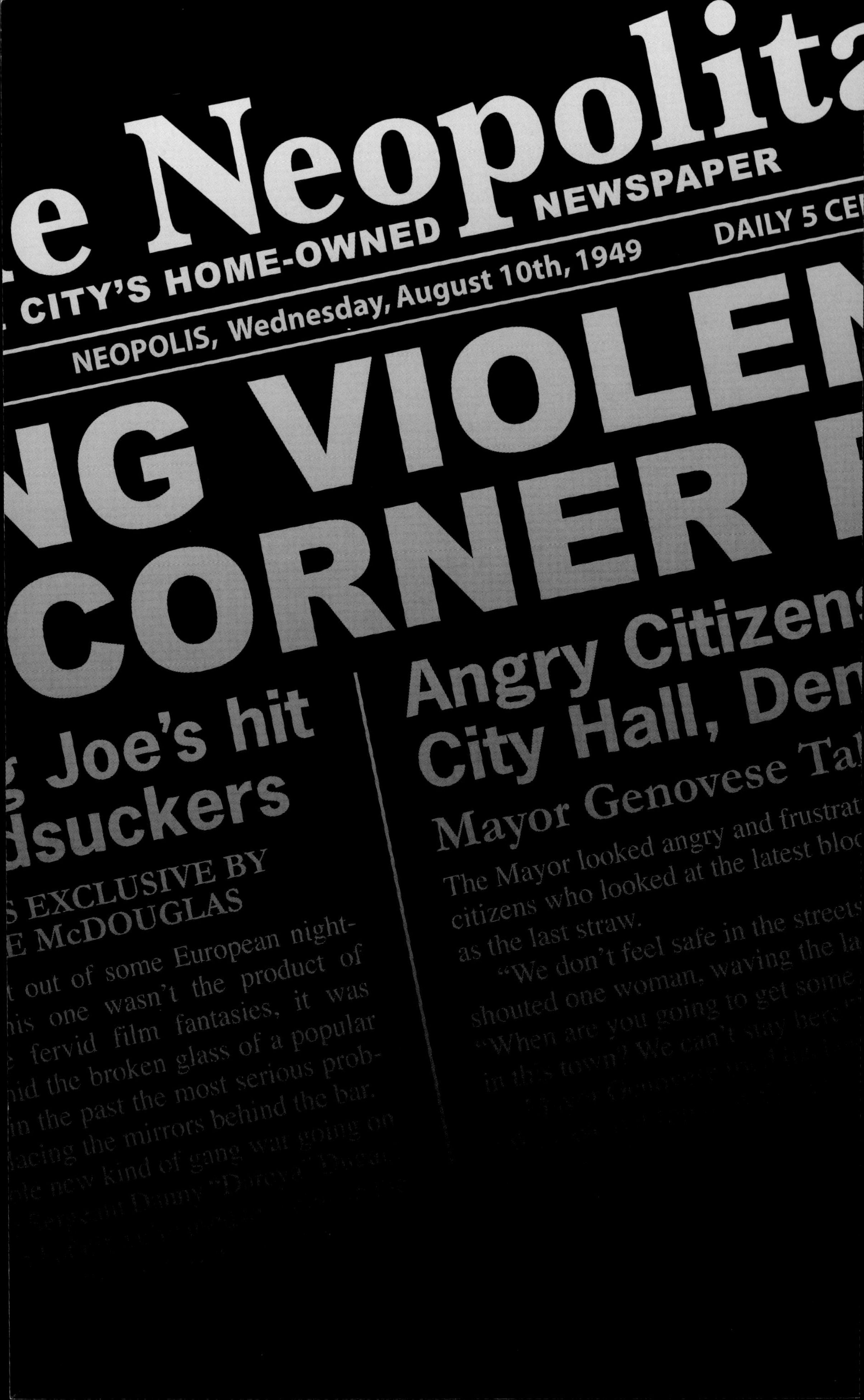

e Neopolita

THE CITY'S HOME-OWNED NEWSPAPER

DAILY 5 CE

NEOPOLIS, Wednesday, August 10th, 1949

NG VIOLEN
CORNER

Joe's hit
dsuckers

S EXCLUSIVE BY
E McDOUGLAS

t out of some European night-
his one wasn't the product of
e fervid film fantasies, it was
nid the broken glass of a popular
n the past the most serious prob-
lacing the mirrors behind the bar.
le new kind of gang war going on
Sergeant Danny "Darryl" Ducas

Angry Citizen
City Hall, Der

Mayor Genovese Tal

The Mayor looked angry and frustrat
citizens who looked at the latest bloc
as the last straw.

"We don't feel safe in the streets
shouted one woman, waving the la
"When are you going to get some
in this town? We can't stay here

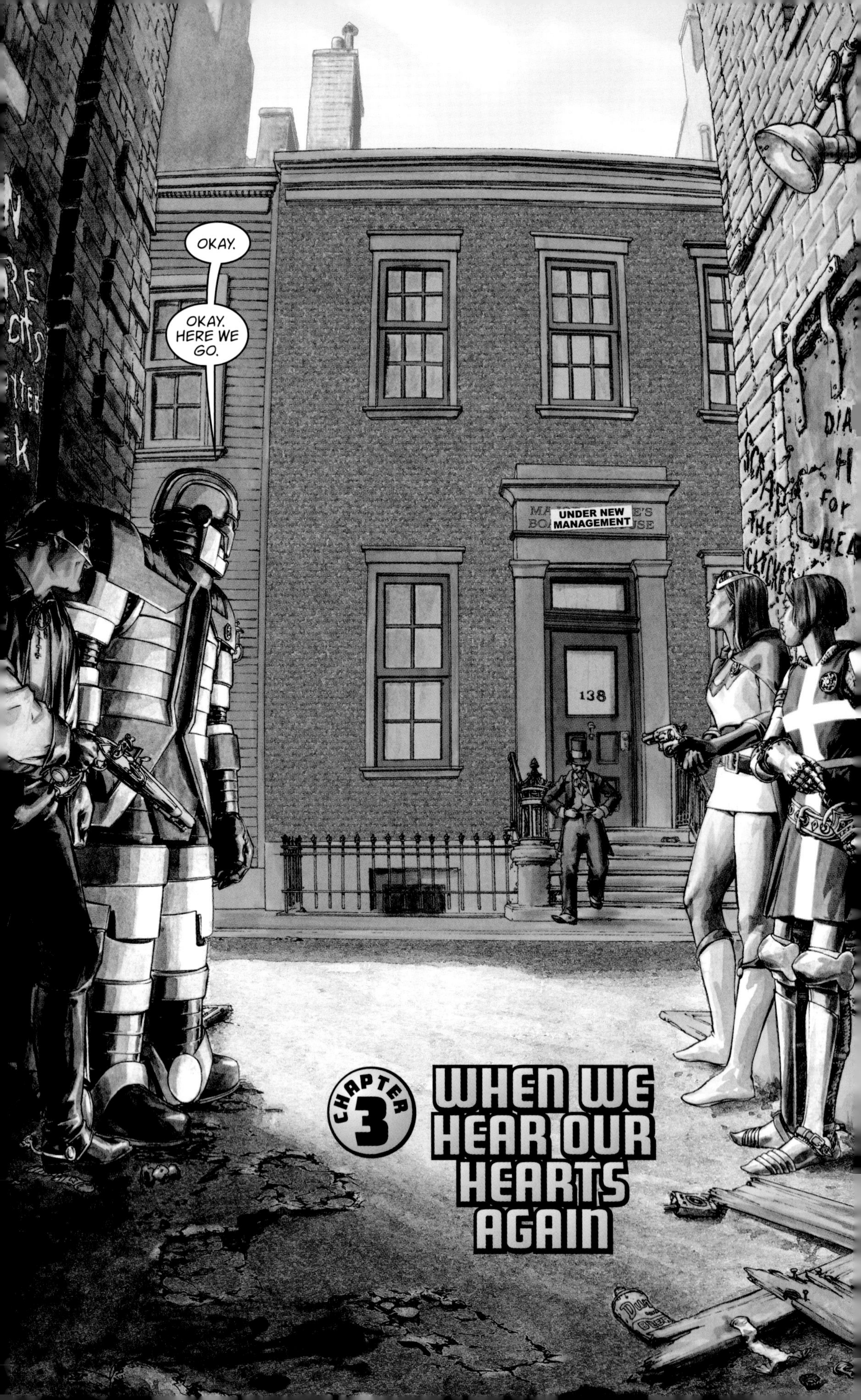
OKAY.
OKAY. HERE WE GO.
UNDER NEW MANAGEMENT
138
CHAPTER 3
WHEN WE HEAR OUR HEARTS AGAIN

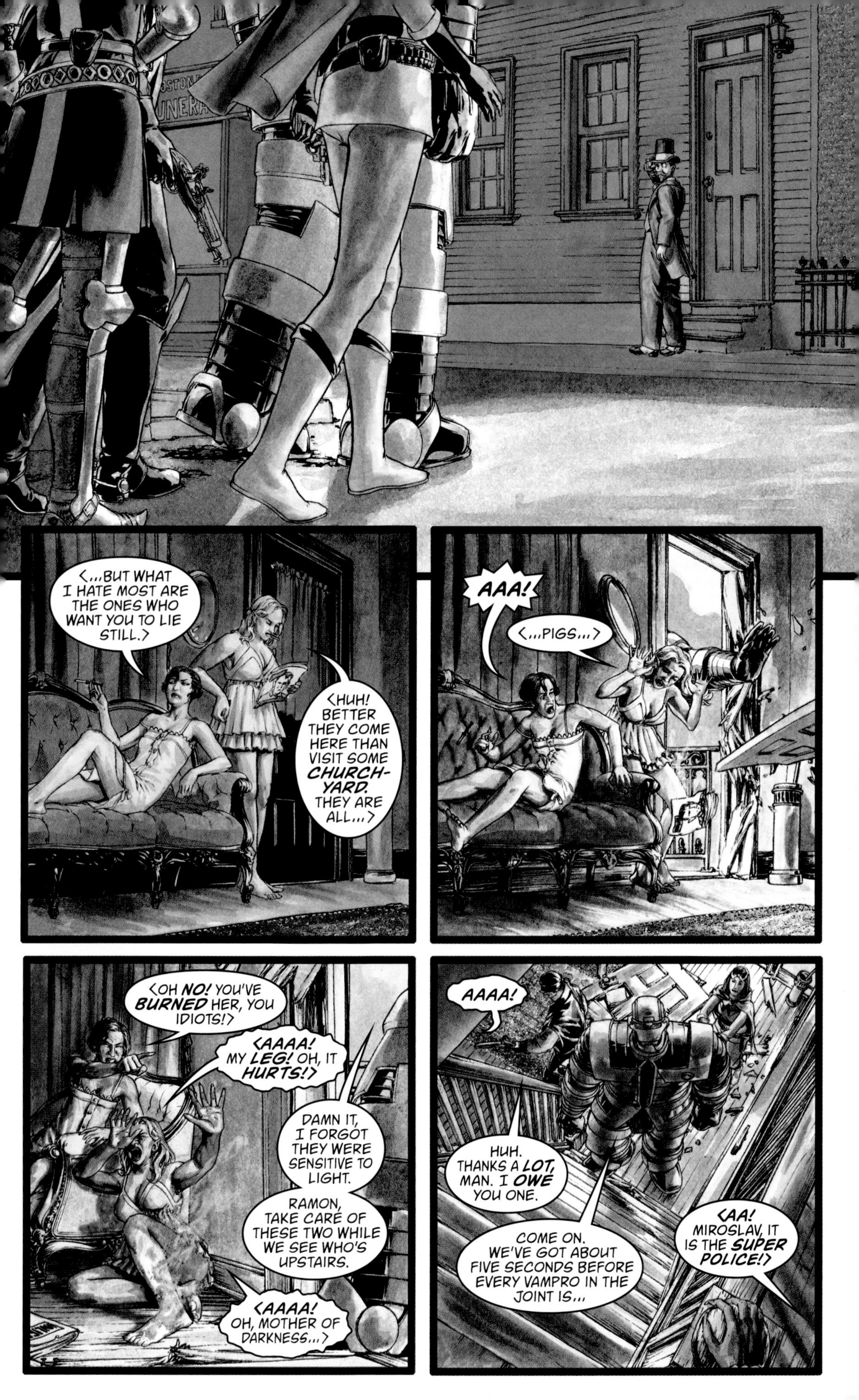
<...BUT WHAT I HATE MOST ARE THE ONES WHO WANT YOU TO LIE STILL.>
<HUH! BETTER THEY COME HERE THAN VISIT SOME **CHURCHYARD.** THEY ARE ALL...>
AAA!
<...PIGS...>
<OH **NO!** YOU'VE **BURNED** HER, YOU IDIOTS!>
<AAAA! MY LEG! OH, IT HURTS!>
DAMN IT, I FORGOT THEY WERE SENSITIVE TO LIGHT.
RAMON, TAKE CARE OF THESE TWO WHILE WE SEE WHO'S UPSTAIRS.
<AAAA! OH, MOTHER OF DARKNESS...>
AAAA!
HUH. THANKS A **LOT,** MAN. I **OWE** YOU ONE.
COME ON. WE'VE GOT ABOUT FIVE SECONDS BEFORE EVERY VAMPRO IN THE JOINT IS...
<AA! MIROSLAV, IT IS THE **SUPER POLICE!>**

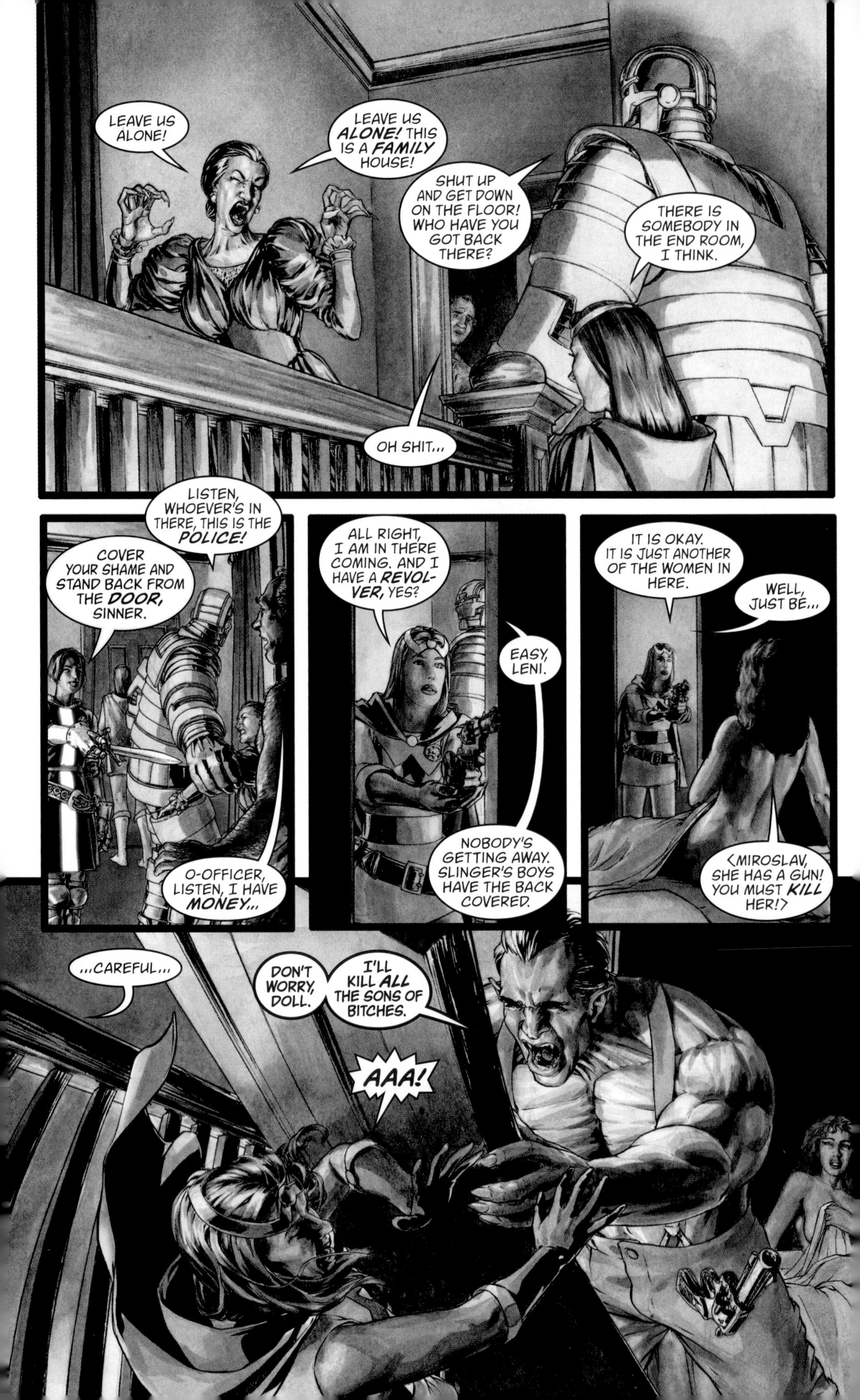
LEAVE US ALONE!
LEAVE US ALONE! THIS IS A FAMILY HOUSE!
SHUT UP AND GET DOWN ON THE FLOOR! WHO HAVE YOU GOT BACK THERE?
THERE IS SOMEBODY IN THE END ROOM, I THINK.
OH SHIT...
LISTEN, WHOEVER'S IN THERE, THIS IS THE POLICE!
COVER YOUR SHAME AND STAND BACK FROM THE DOOR, SINNER.
O-OFFICER, LISTEN, I HAVE MONEY...
ALL RIGHT, I AM IN THERE COMING. AND I HAVE A REVOLVER, YES?
EASY, LENI.
NOBODY'S GETTING AWAY. SLINGER'S BOYS HAVE THE BACK COVERED.
IT IS OKAY. IT IS JUST ANOTHER OF THE WOMEN IN HERE.
WELL, JUST BE...
<MIROSLAV, SHE HAS A GUN! YOU MUST KILL HER!>
...CAREFUL...
DON'T WORRY, DOLL.
I'LL KILL ALL THE SONS OF BITCHES.
AAA!

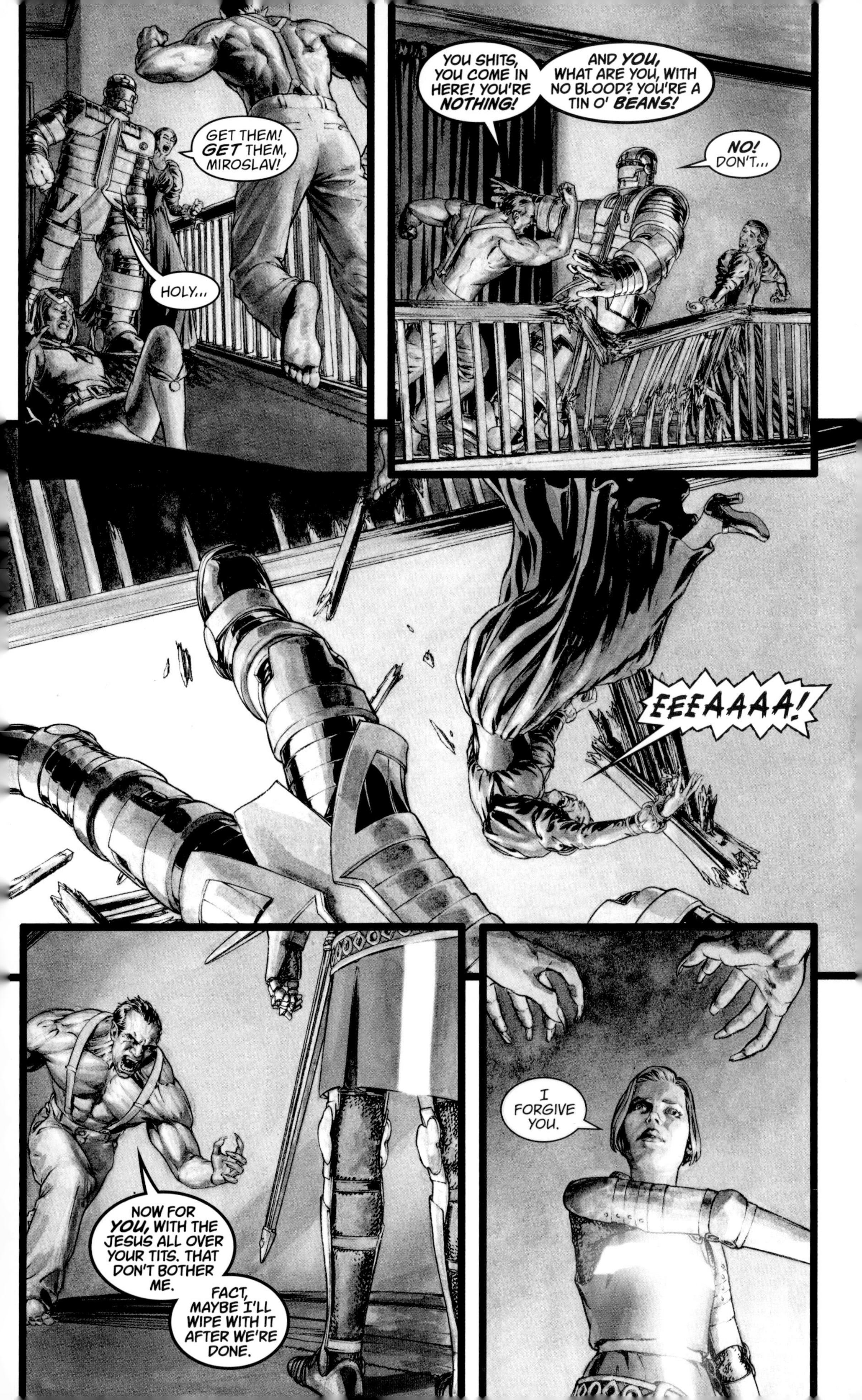
GET THEM! GET THEM, MIROSLAV!
HOLY...
YOU SHITS, YOU COME IN HERE! YOU'RE NOTHING!
AND YOU, WHAT ARE YOU, WITH NO BLOOD? YOU'RE A TIN O' BEANS!
NO! DON'T...
EEEAAAA!
NOW FOR YOU, WITH THE JESUS ALL OVER YOUR TITS. THAT DON'T BOTHER ME.
FACT, MAYBE I'LL WIPE WITH IT AFTER WE'RE DONE.
I FORGIVE YOU.

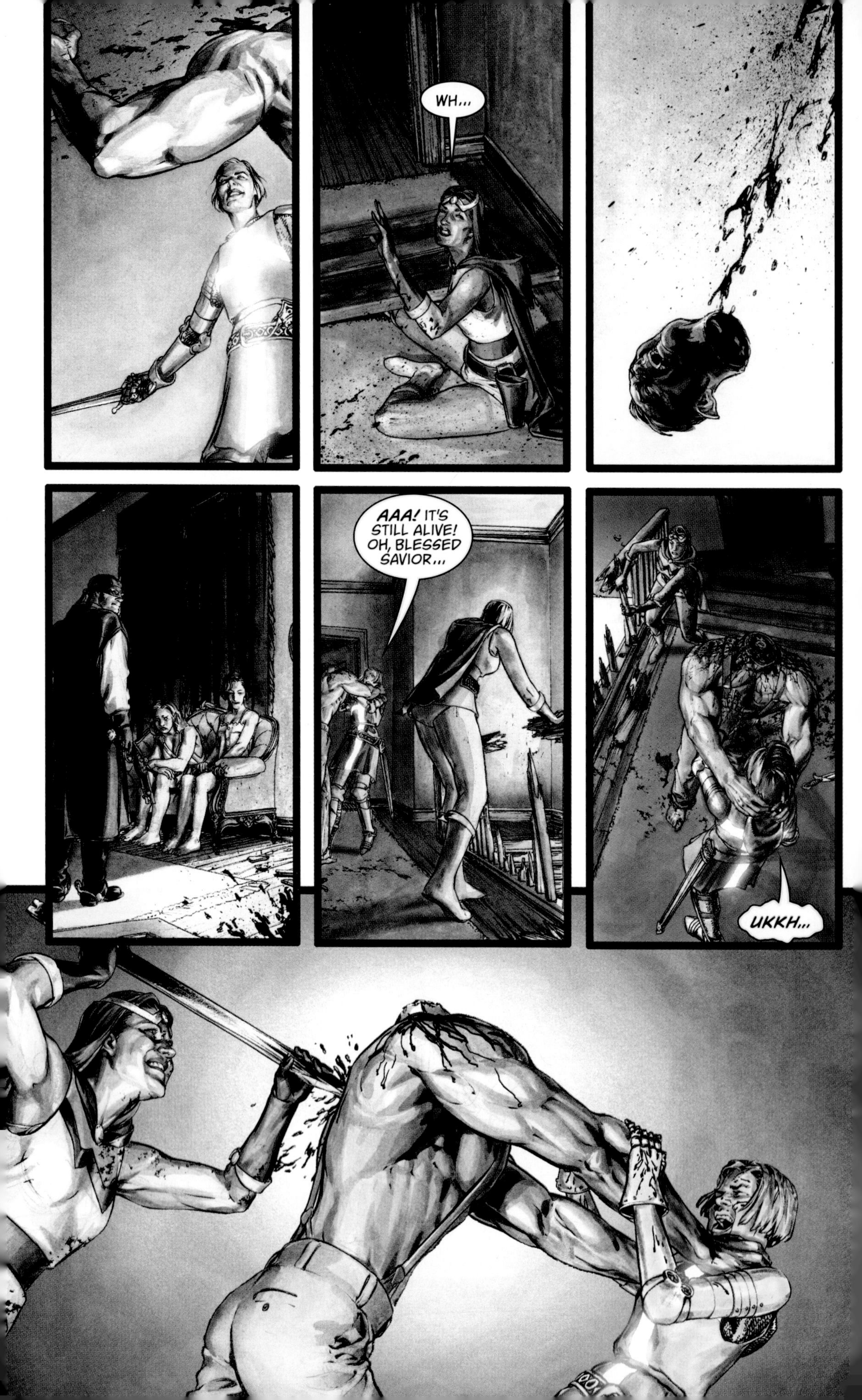
WH...
AAA! IT'S STILL ALIVE! OH, BLESSED SAVIOR...
UKKH...

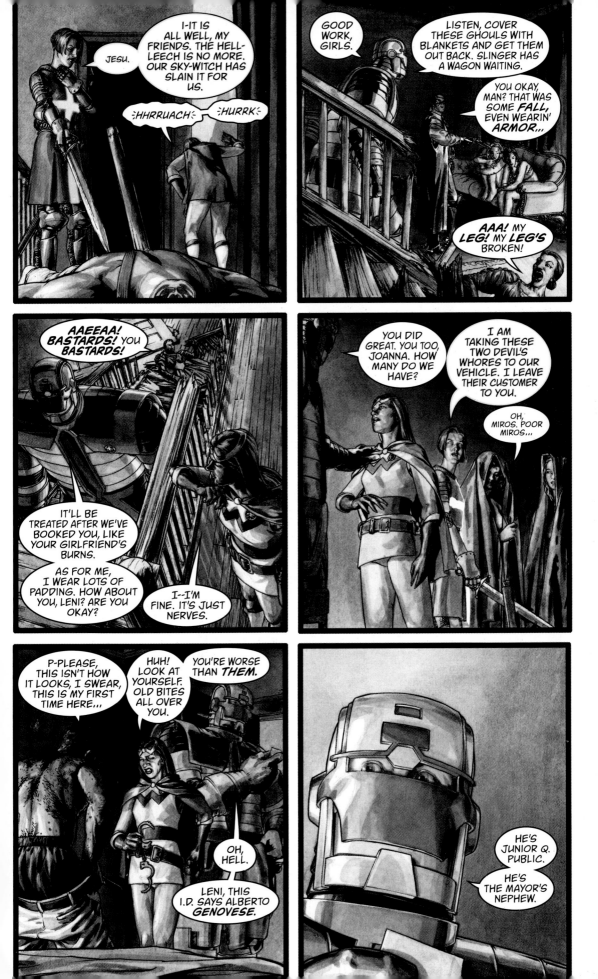

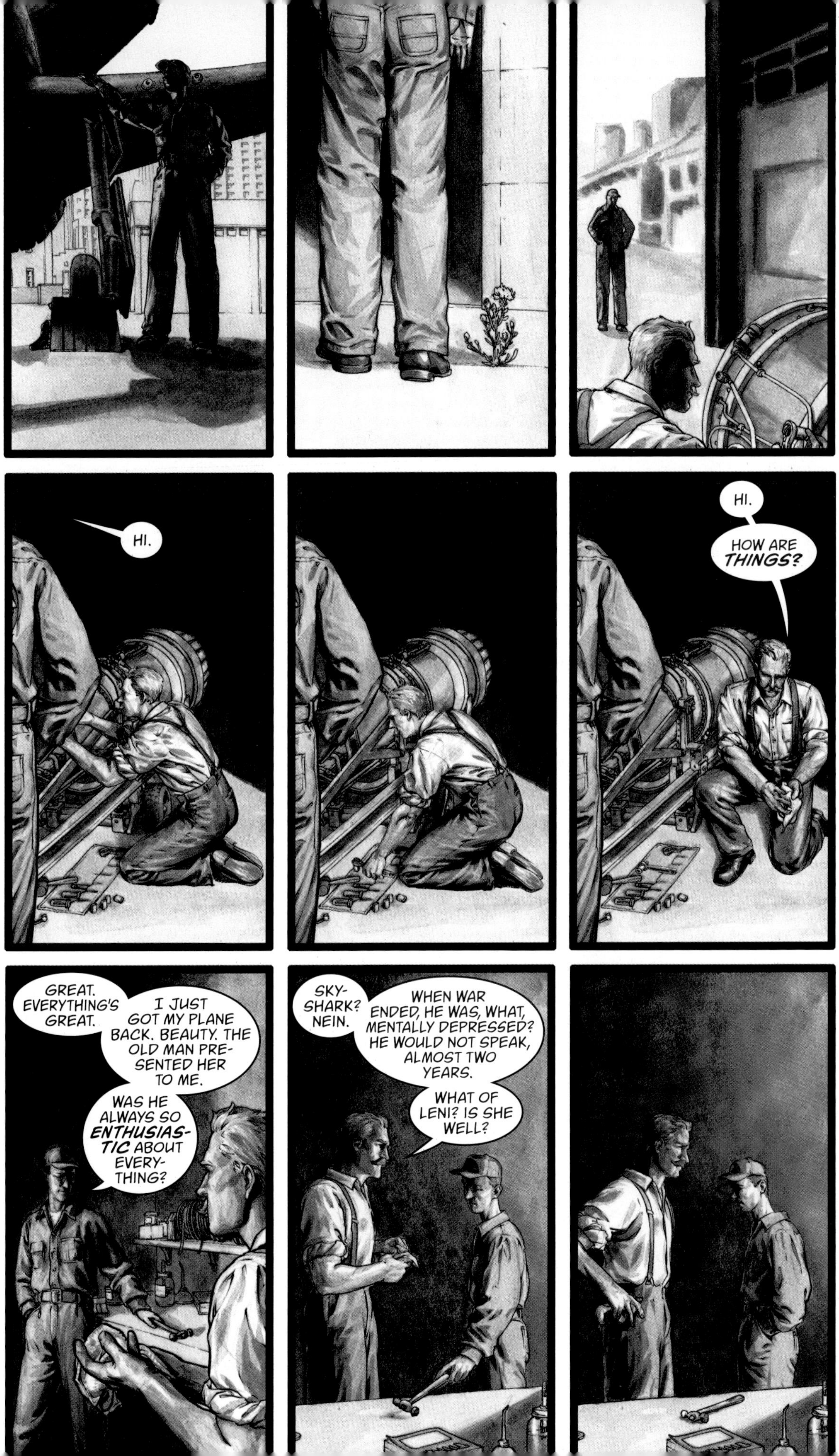
HI.
HI.
HOW ARE *THINGS?*
GREAT. EVERYTHING'S GREAT.
I JUST GOT MY PLANE BACK. BEAUTY. THE OLD MAN PRESENTED HER TO ME.
WAS HE ALWAYS SO *ENTHUSIASTIC* ABOUT EVERYTHING?
SKY-SHARK? NEIN.
WHEN WAR ENDED, HE WAS, WHAT, MENTALLY DEPRESSED? HE WOULD NOT SPEAK, ALMOST TWO YEARS.
WHAT OF LENI? IS SHE WELL?

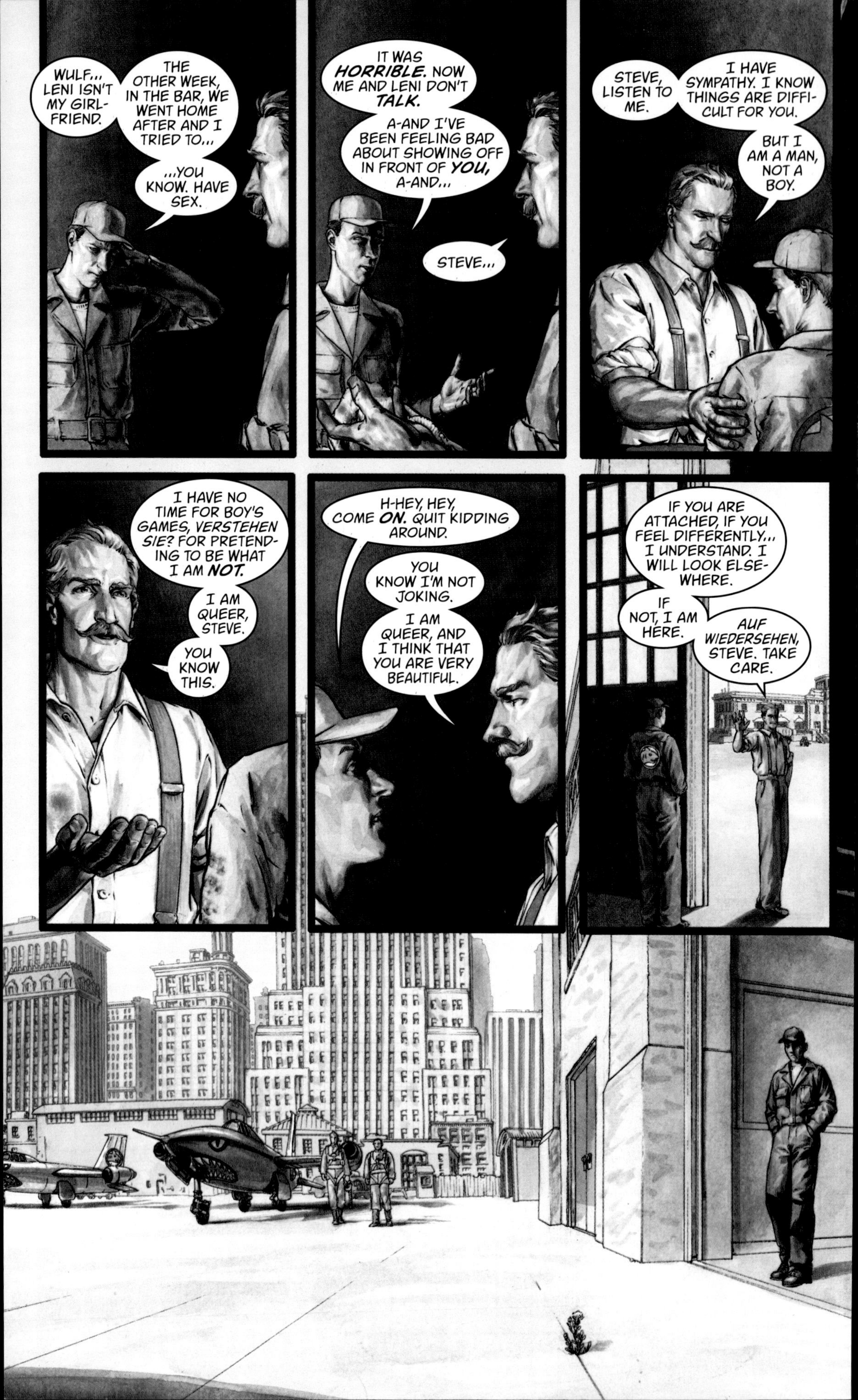
WULF... LENI ISN'T MY GIRL-FRIEND.
THE OTHER WEEK, IN THE BAR, WE WENT HOME AFTER AND I TRIED TO...
...YOU KNOW. HAVE SEX.
IT WAS **HORRIBLE**. NOW ME AND LENI DON'T **TALK**.
A-AND I'VE BEEN FEELING BAD ABOUT SHOWING OFF IN FRONT OF **YOU,** A-AND...
STEVE...
STEVE, LISTEN TO ME.
I HAVE SYMPATHY. I KNOW THINGS ARE DIFFI-CULT FOR YOU.
BUT I AM A MAN, NOT A BOY.
I HAVE NO TIME FOR BOY'S GAMES, *VERSTEHEN SIE?* FOR PRETEND-ING TO BE WHAT I AM **NOT.**
I AM QUEER, STEVE.
YOU KNOW THIS.
H-HEY, HEY, COME **ON**. QUIT KIDDING AROUND.
YOU KNOW I'M NOT JOKING.
I AM QUEER, AND I THINK THAT YOU ARE VERY BEAUTIFUL.
IF YOU ARE ATTACHED, IF YOU FEEL DIFFERENTLY... I UNDERSTAND. I WILL LOOK ELSE-WHERE.
IF NOT, I AM HERE.
AUF WIEDERSEHEN, STEVE. TAKE CARE.

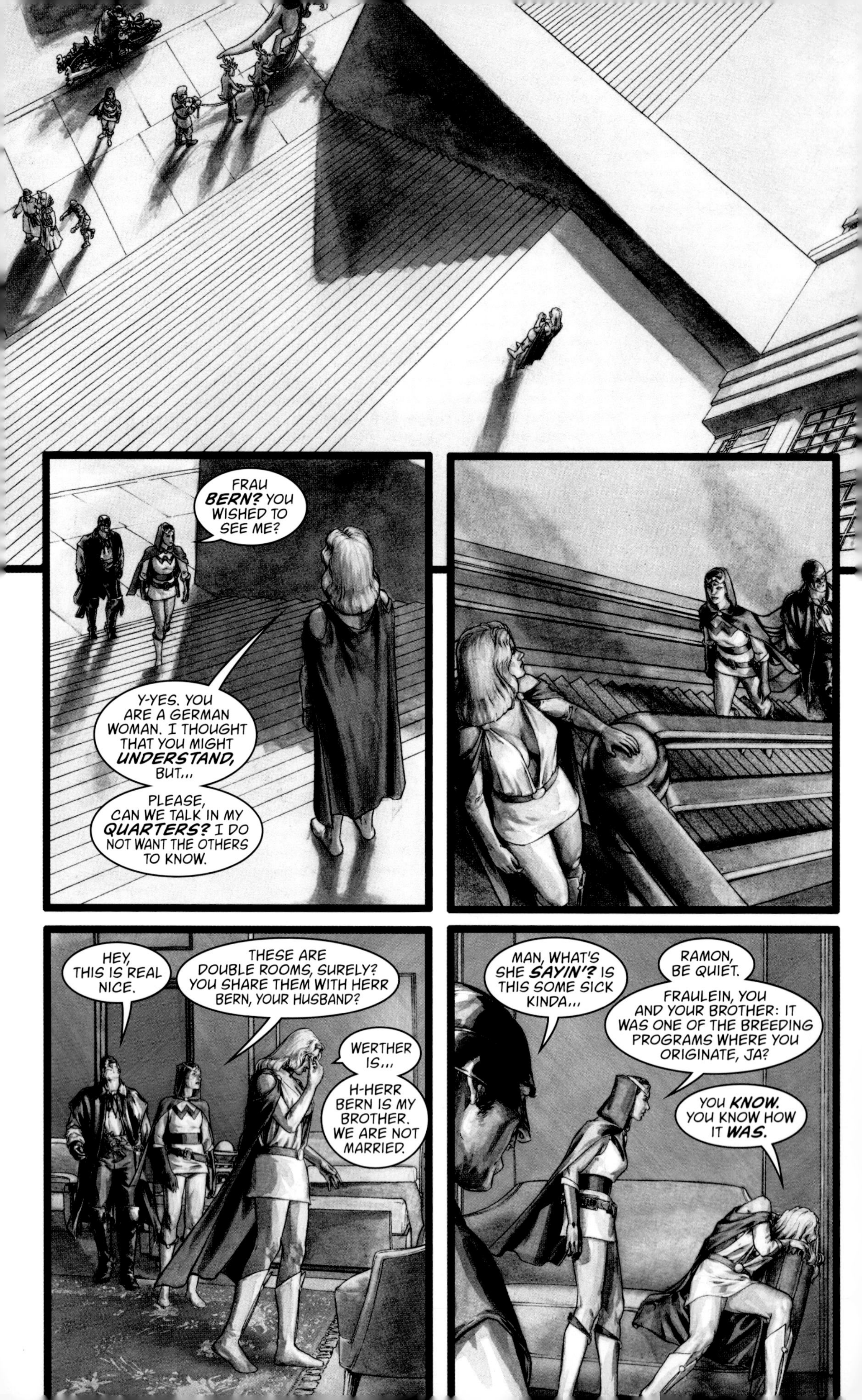
FRAU BERN? YOU WISHED TO SEE ME?
Y-YES. YOU ARE A GERMAN WOMAN. I THOUGHT THAT YOU MIGHT UNDERSTAND, BUT...
PLEASE, CAN WE TALK IN MY QUARTERS? I DO NOT WANT THE OTHERS TO KNOW.
HEY, THIS IS REAL NICE.
THESE ARE DOUBLE ROOMS, SURELY? YOU SHARE THEM WITH HERR BERN, YOUR HUSBAND?
WERTHER IS...
H-HERR BERN IS MY BROTHER. WE ARE NOT MARRIED.
MAN, WHAT'S SHE SAYIN'? IS THIS SOME SICK KINDA...
RAMON, BE QUIET.
FRAULEIN, YOU AND YOUR BROTHER: IT WAS ONE OF THE BREEDING PROGRAMS WHERE YOU ORIGINATE, JA?
YOU KNOW. YOU KNOW HOW IT WAS.

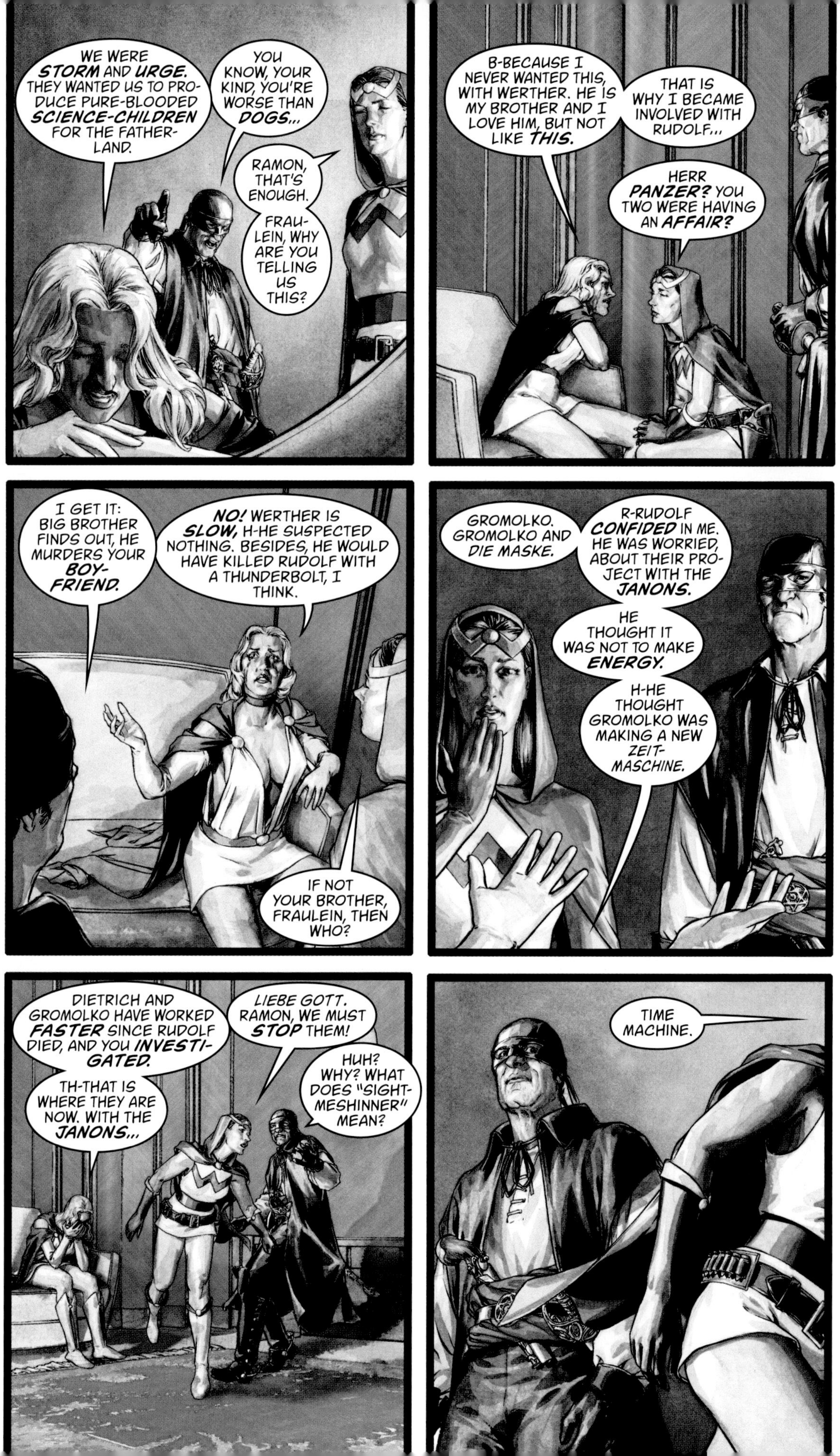
WE WERE STORM AND URGE. THEY WANTED US TO PRODUCE PURE-BLOODED SCIENCE-CHILDREN FOR THE FATHERLAND.
YOU KNOW, YOUR KIND, YOU'RE WORSE THAN DOGS...
RAMON, THAT'S ENOUGH.
FRAULEIN, WHY ARE YOU TELLING US THIS?
B-BECAUSE I NEVER WANTED THIS, WITH WERTHER. HE IS MY BROTHER AND I LOVE HIM, BUT NOT LIKE THIS.
THAT IS WHY I BECAME INVOLVED WITH RUDOLF...
HERR PANZER? YOU TWO WERE HAVING AN AFFAIR?
I GET IT: BIG BROTHER FINDS OUT, HE MURDERS YOUR BOY-FRIEND.
NO! WERTHER IS SLOW, H-HE SUSPECTED NOTHING. BESIDES, HE WOULD HAVE KILLED RUDOLF WITH A THUNDERBOLT, I THINK.
IF NOT YOUR BROTHER, FRAULEIN, THEN WHO?
GROMOLKO. GROMOLKO AND DIE MASKE.
R-RUDOLF CONFIDED IN ME. HE WAS WORRIED, ABOUT THEIR PROJECT WITH THE JANONS.
HE THOUGHT IT WAS NOT TO MAKE ENERGY.
H-HE THOUGHT GROMOLKO WAS MAKING A NEW ZEIT-MASCHINE.
DIETRICH AND GROMOLKO HAVE WORKED FASTER SINCE RUDOLF DIED, AND YOU INVESTIGATED.
TH-THAT IS WHERE THEY ARE NOW. WITH THE JANONS...
LIEBE GOTT. RAMON, WE MUST STOP THEM!
HUH? WHY? WHAT DOES "SIGHT-MESHINNER" MEAN?
TIME MACHINE.

WHAT? WHAT ARE YOU SAYIN'?

I AM SAY-ING, *DU BASTARDE SPANIER,* THAT GUNTER IS IN BERLIN, IN 1943...

...TELLING *DER FUHRER* 1949'S *SECRETS.*

SECRETS? YOU MEAN LIKE THE A-BOMB?

JA. DIE ATOMER BOMBE. THEN THE *FUHRER* CAN MAKE HISTORY *RIGHT* AGAIN.

HE CAN CHANGE THE *FUTURE.*

YOU'RE NUTS. WE *CAUGHT* YOU. THAT AIN'T GONNA *HAPPEN,* MAN.

IT ALREADY *HAS.*

LOOK AT THE *ZEIT-EINFAHRT, MEIN FREUND.* SEE FOR YOURSELF.

politan
EWSPAPER

widely scattered light possible rain to-nite page 9 for more

NEOPOLIS, SUNDAY, AUG. 14, 1949

NAZIS RUN USA

Atque ea diversa penitus dum parte geruntur, irim de caelo misit Saturnia iuno audacem ad turnum. Luco tum forte parentis pilunni turnus sacrata valle sedebat. Ad quem sic osco thaumantias ore t turne, quod omitte

AW, GOD. THAT'S TOMORROW'S *PAPER!*

Y-YOU SAID THIS WAS A DOOR TO THE *PAST...*

THE JANONS GO *BOTH* WAYS IN TIME, *VERSTEHEN SIE?*

BESIDES, THIS WAS OUR FIRST TEST. WE COULD NOT PREDICT THE EFFECTS.

BUT NOW, I THINK, THE PREDICTION, IT IS VERY *CLEAR, NICHT WAHR?*

GUNTER HAS ALREADY *SUCCEEDED,* AND YOUR LITTLE TURNCOAT *PARTNER* HAS JUST AS CLEARLY *FAILED.*

SHE PROBABLY LIES DEAD.

IN BERLIN.

SIX YEARS AGO.

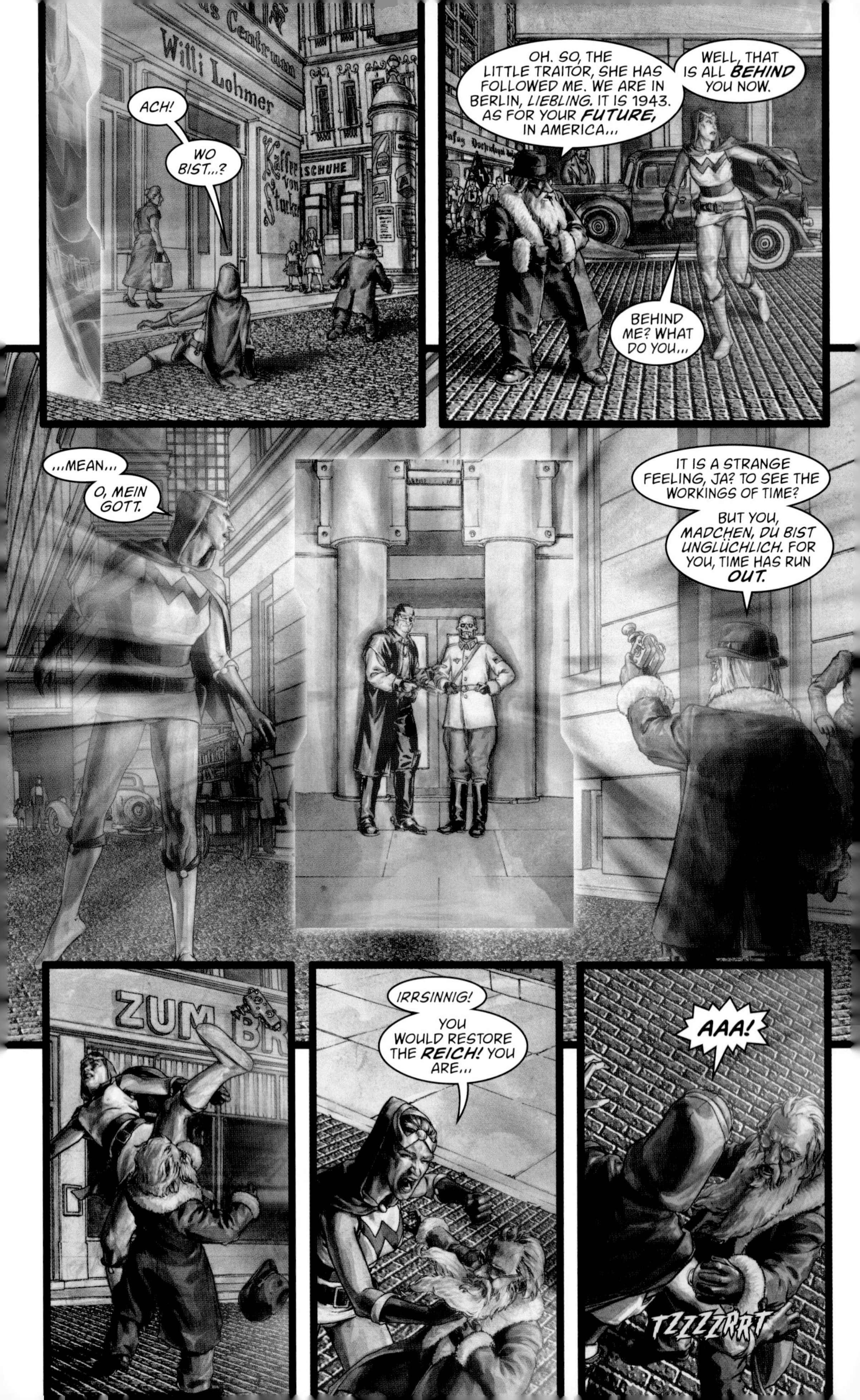
Willi Lohmer
Centrum
SCHUHE
ACH!
WO BIST...?
OH. SO, THE LITTLE TRAITOR, SHE HAS FOLLOWED ME. WE ARE IN BERLIN, *LIEBLING.* IT IS 1943. AS FOR YOUR ***FUTURE,*** IN AMERICA...
WELL, THAT IS ALL ***BEHIND*** YOU NOW.
BEHIND ME? WHAT DO YOU...
...MEAN...
O, MEIN GOTT.
IT IS A STRANGE FEELING, JA? TO SEE THE WORKINGS OF TIME?
BUT YOU, *MADCHEN, DU BIST UNGLÜCHLICH.* FOR YOU, TIME HAS RUN ***OUT.***
ZUM BR
IRRSINNIG!
YOU WOULD RESTORE THE ***REICH!*** YOU ARE...
AAA!
TZZZZRRT

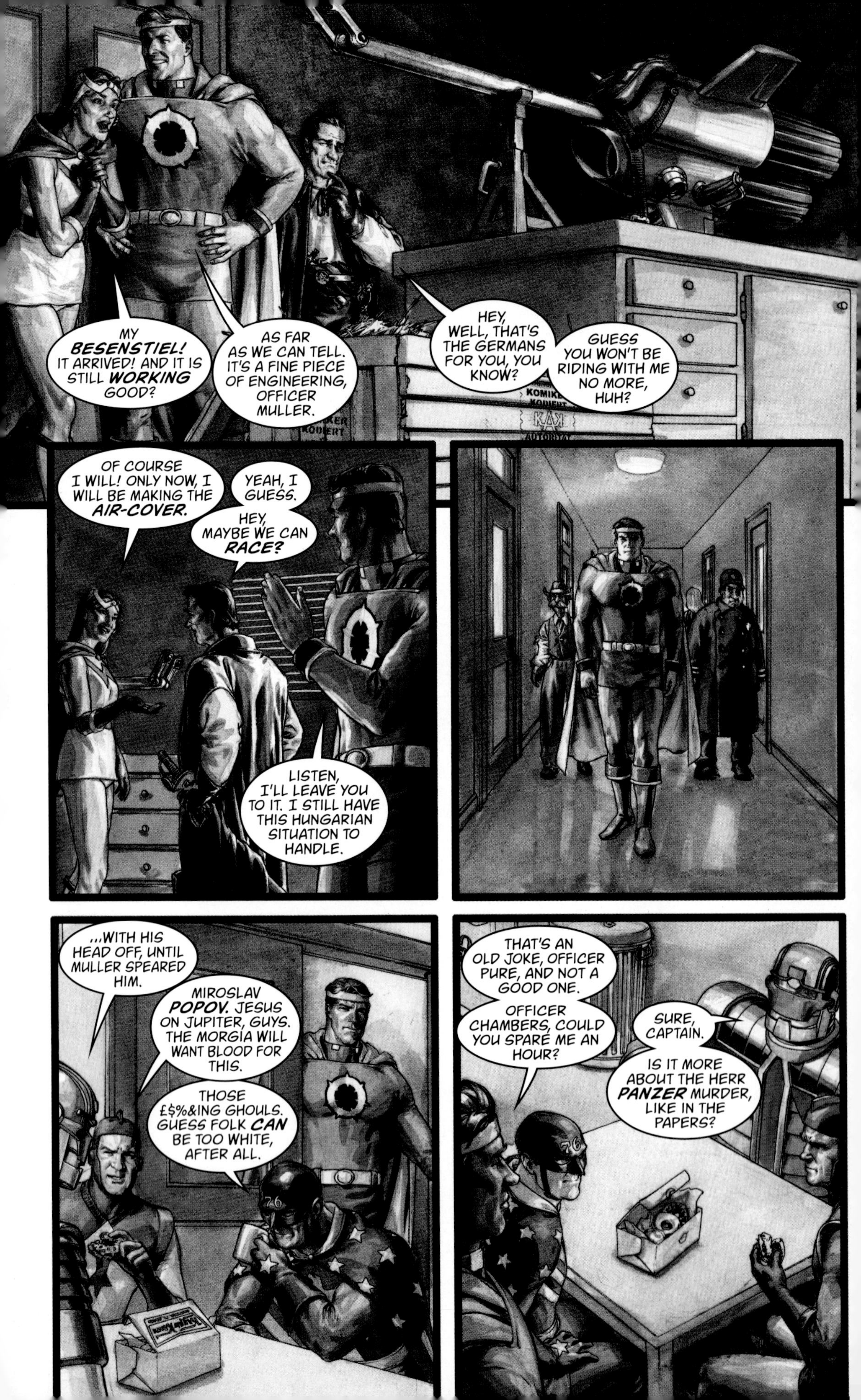

MY BESENSTIEL! IT ARRIVED! AND IT IS STILL WORKING GOOD?
AS FAR AS WE CAN TELL. IT'S A FINE PIECE OF ENGINEERING, OFFICER MULLER.
HEY, WELL, THAT'S THE GERMANS FOR YOU, YOU KNOW?
GUESS YOU WON'T BE RIDING WITH ME NO MORE, HUH?
OF COURSE I WILL! ONLY NOW, I WILL BE MAKING THE AIR-COVER.
YEAH, I GUESS.
HEY, MAYBE WE CAN RACE?
LISTEN, I'LL LEAVE YOU TO IT. I STILL HAVE THIS HUNGARIAN SITUATION TO HANDLE.
...WITH HIS HEAD OFF, UNTIL MULLER SPEARED HIM.
MIROSLAV POPOV. JESUS ON JUPITER, GUYS. THE MORGIA WILL WANT BLOOD FOR THIS.
THOSE £$%&ING GHOULS. GUESS FOLK CAN BE TOO WHITE, AFTER ALL.
THAT'S AN OLD JOKE, OFFICER PURE, AND NOT A GOOD ONE.
OFFICER CHAMBERS, COULD YOU SPARE ME AN HOUR?
SURE, CAPTAIN.
IS IT MORE ABOUT THE HERR PANZER MURDER, LIKE IN THE PAPERS?

Panel 1:
NO. NO, WE THINK WE HAVE THAT PRETTY MUCH FIGURED.

PANZER FOUND OUT ABOUT GROMOLKO'S PLAN, SO GROMOLKO KILLED HIM.

ADMINISTERED SOME FLESH-EATING AGENT THROUGH HIS ARMOR'S *VENTS*. GUESS THAT'S PROBABLY YOUR ULTIMATE *NIGHTMARE*.

Panel 2:
WHAT?

OH...YES. YES, THAT SCARES THE YOU-KNOW-WHAT OUT OF ME.

SO IF IT'S NOT THE GROMOLKO MANHUNT, WHAT IS IT?

MIROSLAV *POPOV*. WE'VE HAD A PHONE TIP-OFF CONCERNING HUNGARIAN *GANGSTER* ACTIVITY.

Panel 3:
WHAT KIND?

MIROSLAV'S KIND: VAMPIRE PROSTITUTION. THEY INFECT ORDINARY WOMEN, WHO ARE THEN BLOOD-ADDICTS AND THUS EASY TO TURN OUT.

OUR SOURCE TELLS US A NEW ORGANIZER, TO REPLACE MIROSLAV, IS ARRIVING ON SATURDAY.

Panel 4:
WE CAN INTERCEPT HIM, CAPTAIN. JUST TELL US WHERE THIS CREEP IS SHOWING UP...

NEOPOLIS CENTRAL, ELEVEN PM ON SATURDAY NIGHT.

EXCEPT IT ISN'T THAT SIMPLE.

FOR ONE THING, THIS GUY'S LIKELY TO BRING *REINFORCEMENTS*.

Panel 5:
YES. YES, I SUPPOSE SO, AFTER WHAT HAPPENED TO MIROSLAV.

STILL, CAN'T WE JUST GO IN HEAVY-HANDED?

YES. YES, THAT'S A POSSIBILITY.

COME ON. LET'S RIDE OVER THERE NOW AND TAKE A LOOK.

NEOPOLIS POLICE

Panel 6:
Dagwoods

RAD

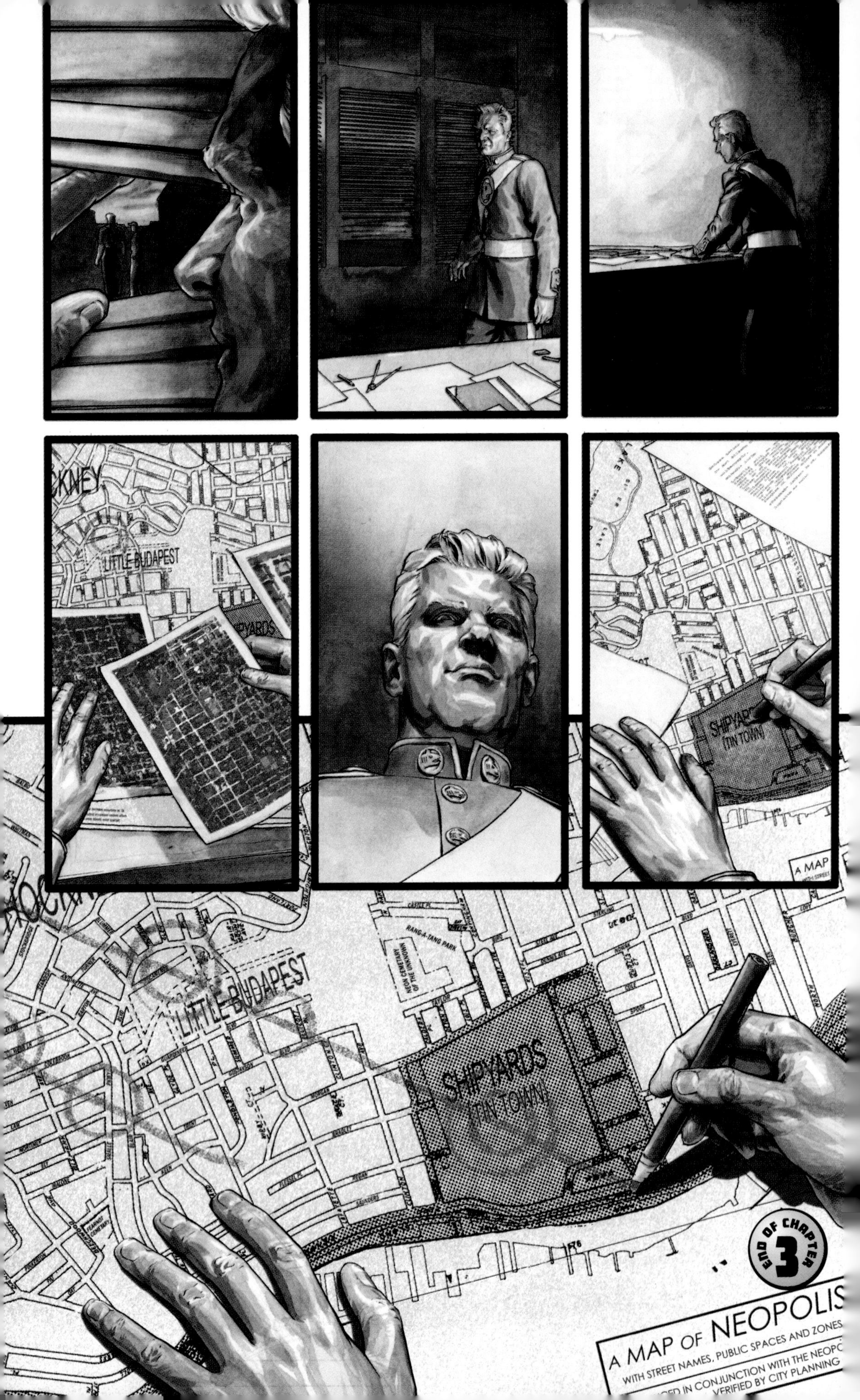

LITTLE BUDAPEST
SHIPYARDS (TIN TOWN)
RANG-A-TANG PARK
NEON CEMETARY OF THE UNKNOWN
END OF CHAPTER 3
A MAP OF NEOPOLIS
WITH STREET NAMES, PUBLIC SPACES AND ZONES

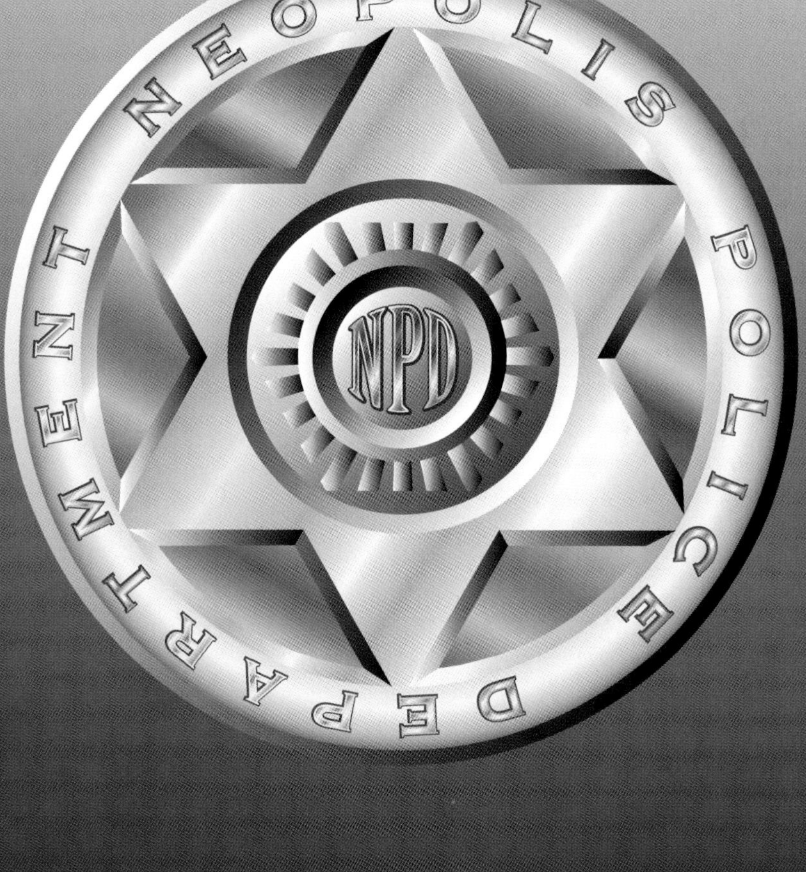
NEOPOLIS POLICE DEPARTMENT
NPD

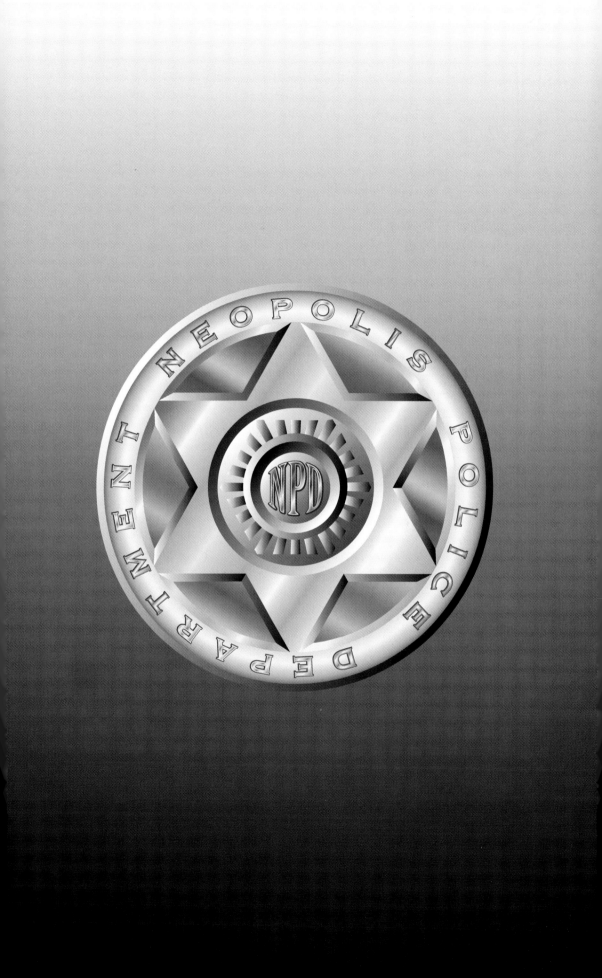

...e Neopolit...

...E CITY'S HOME-OWNED NEWSPAPER

NEOPOLIS, Friday, August 19th, 1949

DAILY 5 C...

...VERED PO...
...KING ARR...

...Have Equal
...New Force

...IS EXCLUSIVE BY
...DA LEDBETTER

...covered by the Neopolis Police
...diabolical plot to restore to power
...n with some sort of time machine,
...arge part by a German immigrant,
...opposing side in the war, now just
... desire to right the wrongs that were
...ople as well as the citizens of the
...ller is one of a new breed of officers
...

Military Optio...
Considered i...

Commander-in-Chi...

The President of the United States h...
opinion that many citizens from oth...
these new threats can only be hand...
reluctant to take steps that are not...
local government, which is still in...
period of adjustment. But someti...
to counter the attacks on private...
make Neopolis a lawless cit...
and put an...

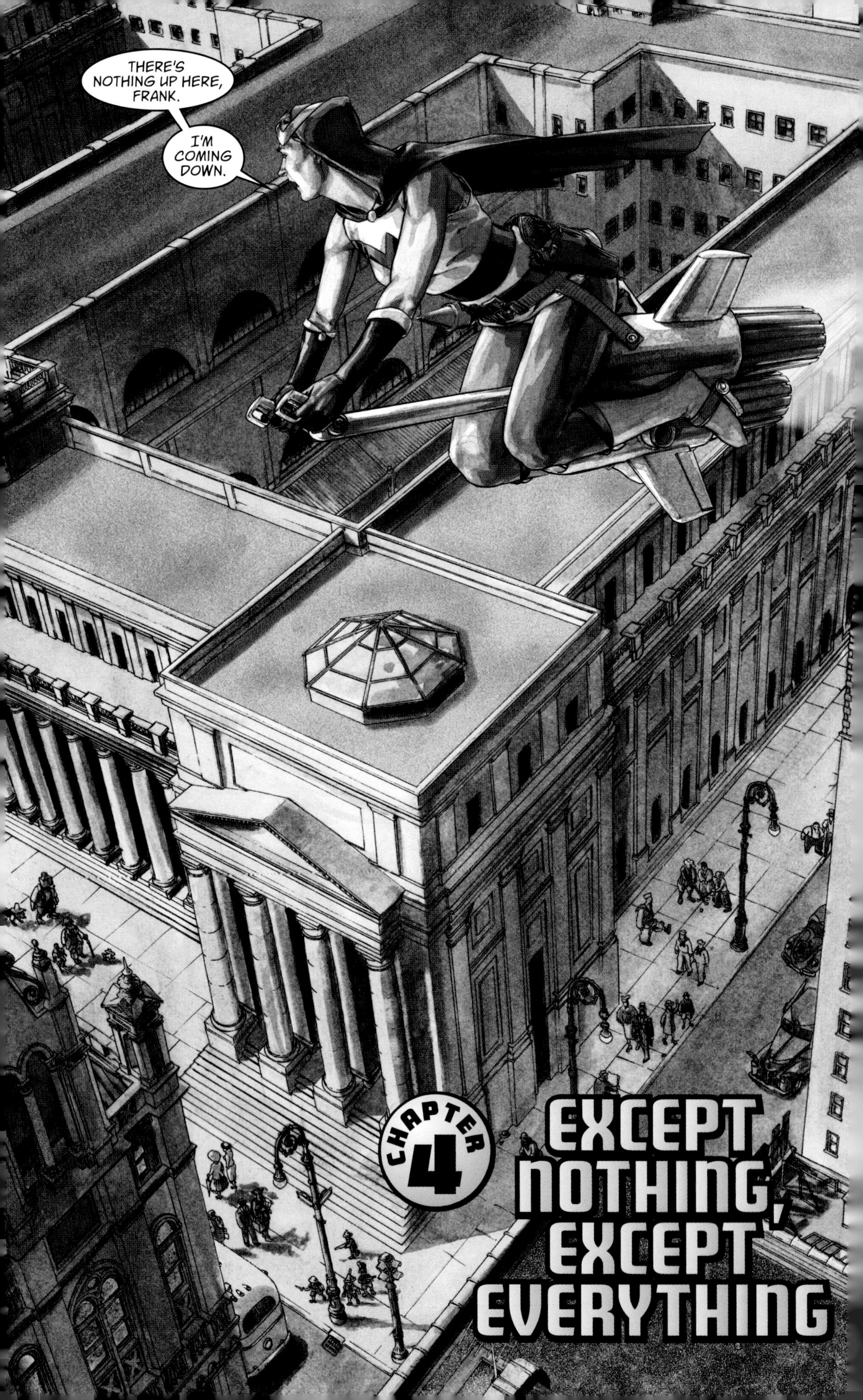
THERE'S NOTHING UP HERE, FRANK.
I'M COMING DOWN.
CHAPTER 4
EXCEPT NOTHING, EXCEPT EVERYTHING

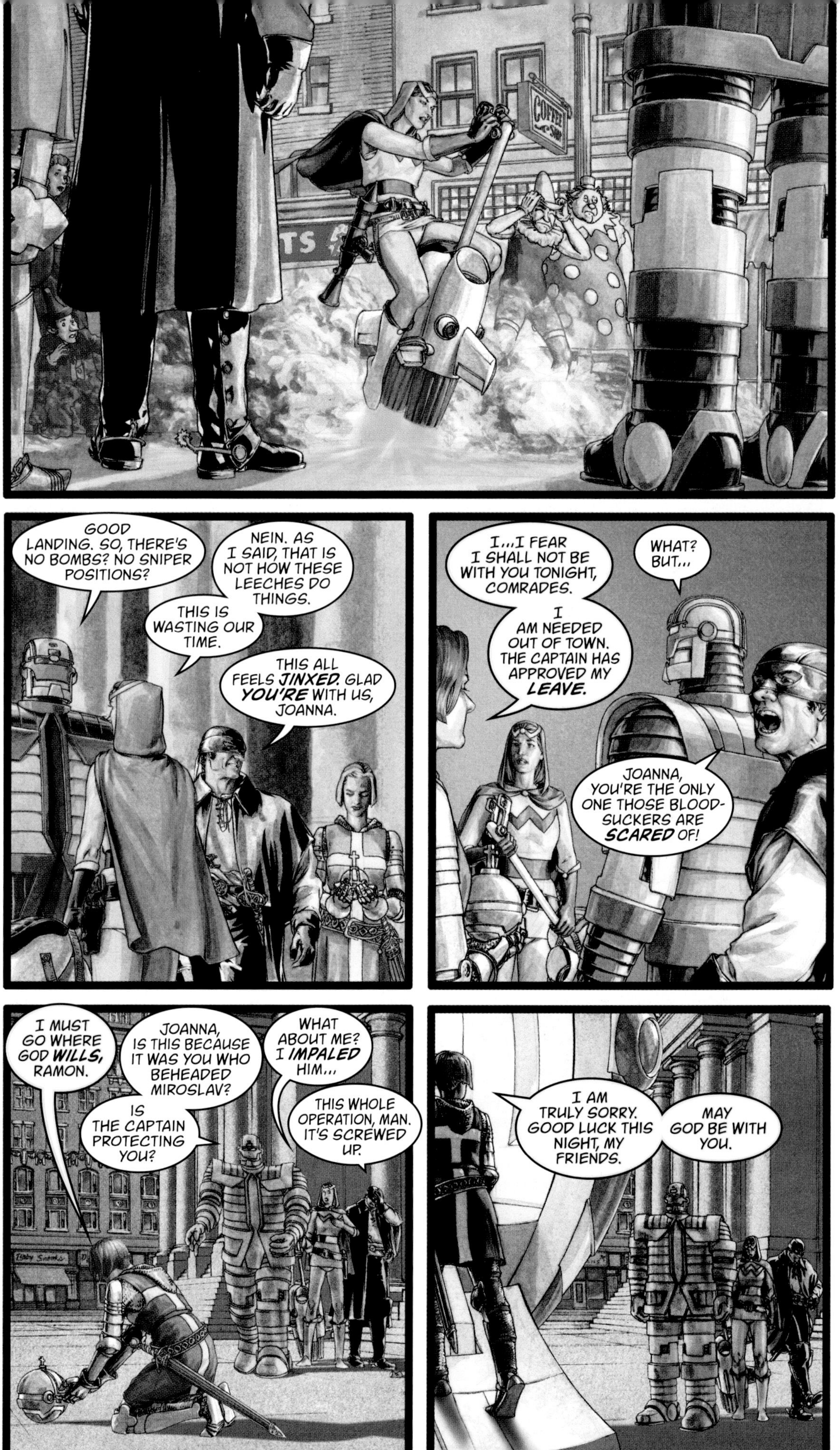

COFFEE SHOP
GOOD LANDING. SO, THERE'S NO BOMBS? NO SNIPER POSITIONS?
NEIN. AS I SAID, THAT IS NOT HOW THESE LEECHES DO THINGS.
THIS IS WASTING OUR TIME.
THIS ALL FEELS *JINXED*. GLAD *YOU'RE* WITH US, JOANNA.
I...I FEAR I SHALL NOT BE WITH YOU TONIGHT, COMRADES.
WHAT? BUT...
I AM NEEDED OUT OF TOWN. THE CAPTAIN HAS APPROVED MY *LEAVE*.
JOANNA, YOU'RE THE ONLY ONE THOSE BLOOD-SUCKERS ARE *SCARED* OF!
I MUST GO WHERE GOD *WILLS*, RAMON.
JOANNA, IS THIS BECAUSE IT WAS YOU WHO BEHEADED MIROSLAV?
IS THE CAPTAIN PROTECTING YOU?
WHAT ABOUT ME? I *IMPALED* HIM...
THIS WHOLE OPERATION, MAN. IT'S SCREWED UP.
I AM TRULY SORRY. GOOD LUCK THIS NIGHT, MY FRIENDS.
MAY GOD BE WITH YOU.

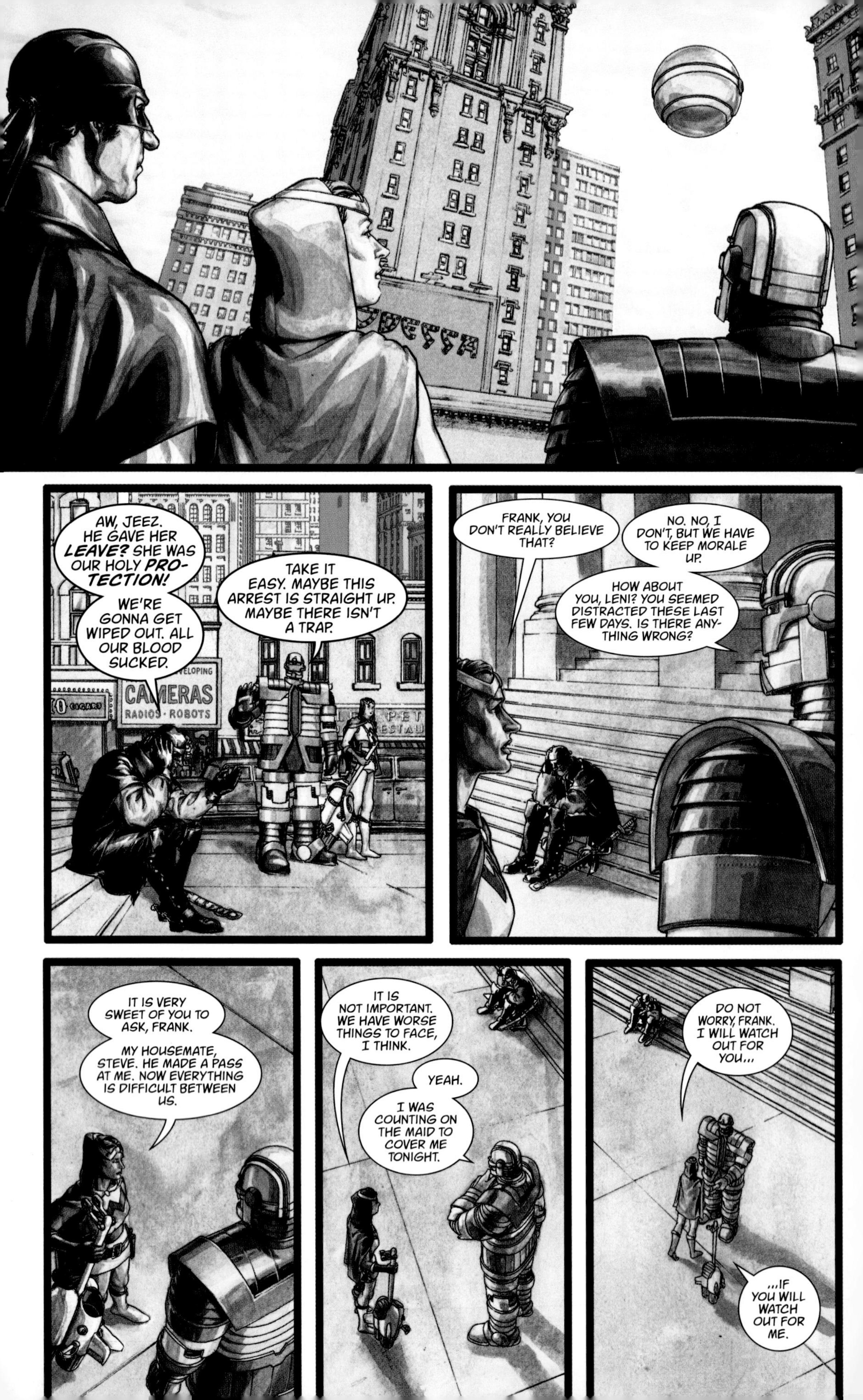

AW, JEEZ. HE GAVE HER LEAVE? SHE WAS OUR HOLY PRO-TECTION!
WE'RE GONNA GET WIPED OUT. ALL OUR BLOOD SUCKED.
TAKE IT EASY. MAYBE THIS ARREST IS STRAIGHT UP. MAYBE THERE ISN'T A TRAP.
CAMERAS
RADIOS · ROBOTS
FRANK, YOU DON'T REALLY BELIEVE THAT?
NO. NO, I DON'T, BUT WE HAVE TO KEEP MORALE UP.
HOW ABOUT YOU, LENI? YOU SEEMED DISTRACTED THESE LAST FEW DAYS. IS THERE ANY-THING WRONG?
IT IS VERY SWEET OF YOU TO ASK, FRANK.
MY HOUSEMATE, STEVE. HE MADE A PASS AT ME. NOW EVERYTHING IS DIFFICULT BETWEEN US.
IT IS NOT IMPORTANT. WE HAVE WORSE THINGS TO FACE, I THINK.
YEAH.
I WAS COUNTING ON THE MAID TO COVER ME TONIGHT.
DO NOT WORRY, FRANK. I WILL WATCH OUT FOR YOU...
...IF YOU WILL WATCH OUT FOR ME.

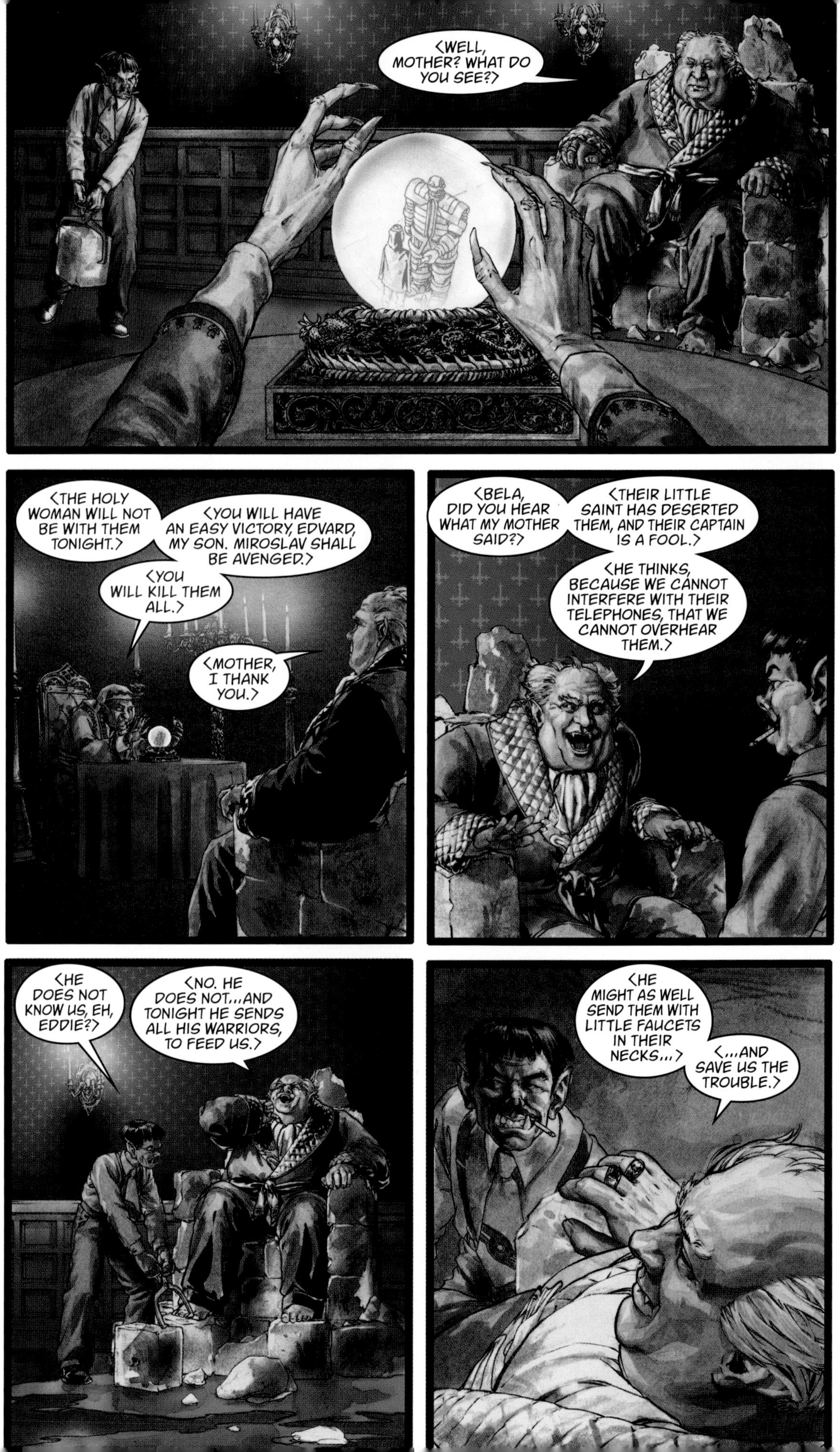
<WELL, MOTHER? WHAT DO YOU SEE?>
<THE HOLY WOMAN WILL NOT BE WITH THEM TONIGHT.>
<YOU WILL HAVE AN EASY VICTORY, EDVARD, MY SON. MIROSLAV SHALL BE AVENGED.>
<YOU WILL KILL THEM ALL.>
<MOTHER, I THANK YOU.>
<BELA, DID YOU HEAR WHAT MY MOTHER SAID?>
<THEIR LITTLE SAINT HAS DESERTED THEM, AND THEIR CAPTAIN IS A FOOL.>
<HE THINKS, BECAUSE WE CANNOT INTERFERE WITH THEIR TELEPHONES, THAT WE CANNOT OVERHEAR THEM.>
<HE DOES NOT KNOW US, EH, EDDIE?>
<NO. HE DOES NOT...AND TONIGHT HE SENDS ALL HIS WARRIORS, TO FEED US.>
<HE MIGHT AS WELL SEND THEM WITH LITTLE FAUCETS IN THEIR NECKS...>
<...AND SAVE US THE TROUBLE.>

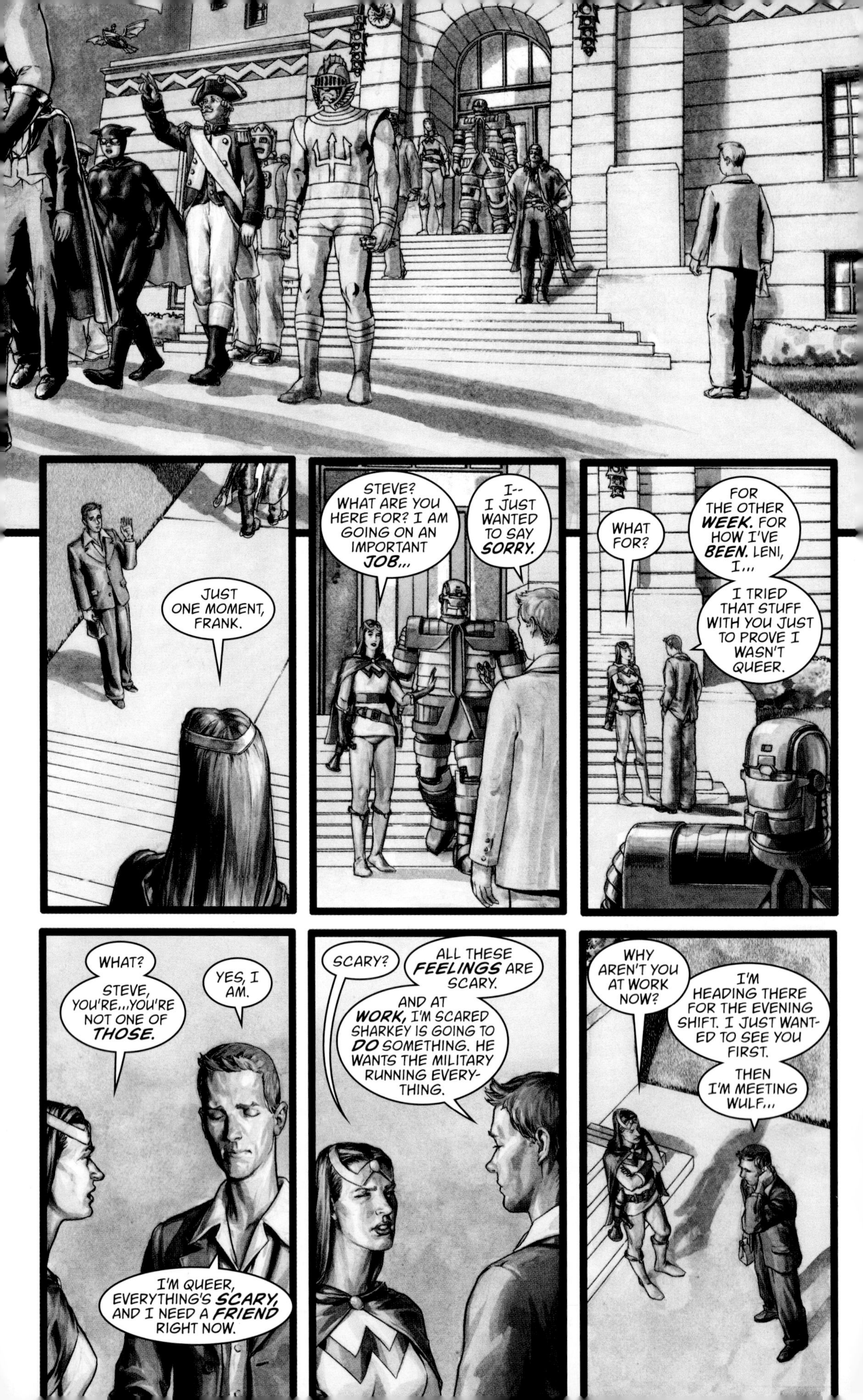
JUST ONE MOMENT, FRANK.
STEVE? WHAT ARE YOU HERE FOR? I AM GOING ON AN IMPORTANT JOB...
I-- I JUST WANTED TO SAY SORRY.
WHAT FOR?
FOR THE OTHER WEEK. FOR HOW I'VE BEEN. LENI, I...
I TRIED THAT STUFF WITH YOU JUST TO PROVE I WASN'T QUEER.
WHAT?
STEVE, YOU'RE...YOU'RE NOT ONE OF THOSE.
YES, I AM.
I'M QUEER, EVERYTHING'S SCARY, AND I NEED A FRIEND RIGHT NOW.
SCARY?
ALL THESE FEELINGS ARE SCARY.
AND AT WORK, I'M SCARED SHARKEY IS GOING TO DO SOMETHING. HE WANTS THE MILITARY RUNNING EVERY-THING.
WHY AREN'T YOU AT WORK NOW?
I'M HEADING THERE FOR THE EVENING SHIFT. I JUST WANT-ED TO SEE YOU FIRST.
THEN I'M MEETING WULF...

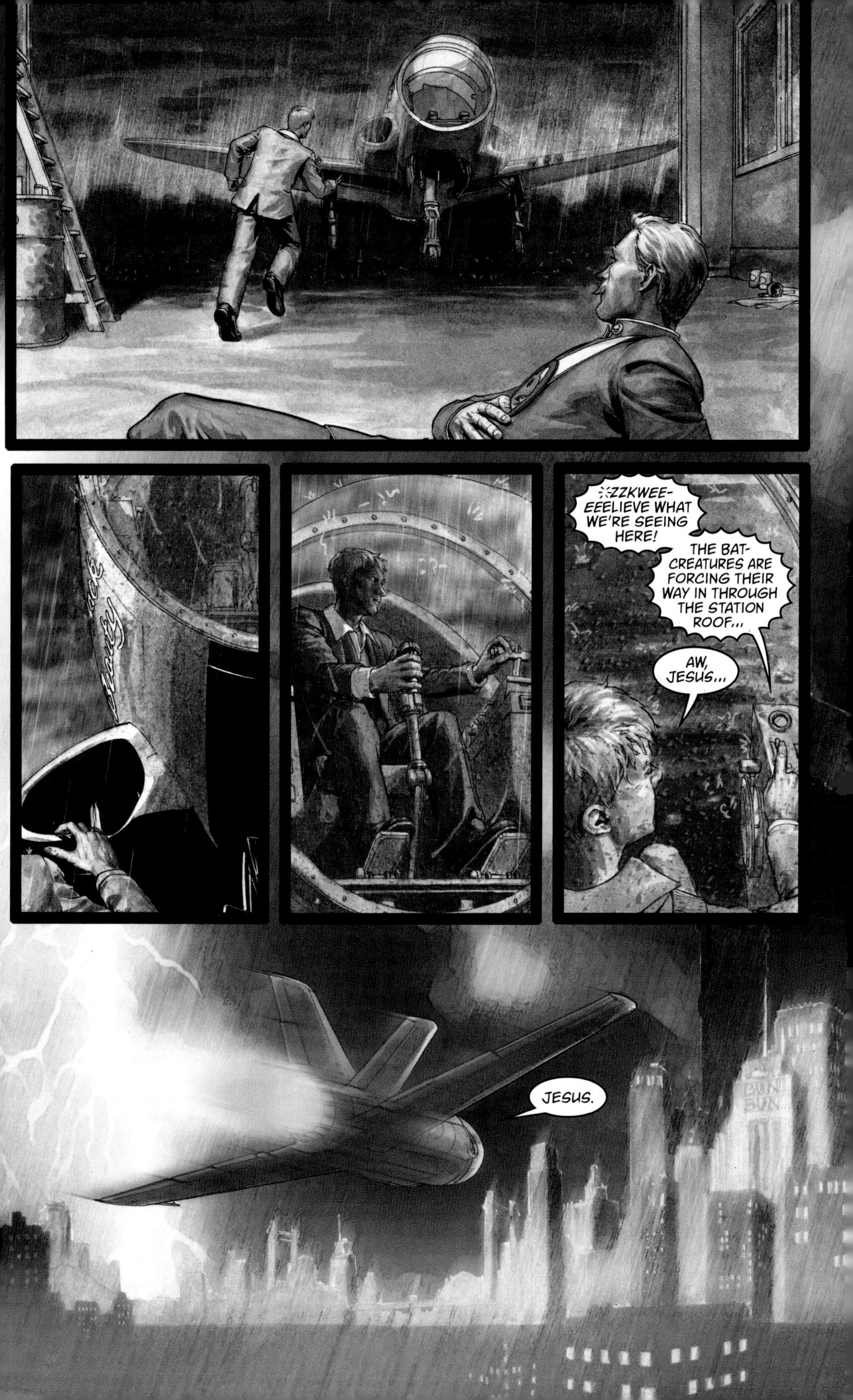
ZZKWEE-
EEELIEVE WHAT WE'RE SEEING HERE!
THE BAT-CREATURES ARE FORCING THEIR WAY IN THROUGH THE STATION ROOF...
AW, JESUS...
JESUS.

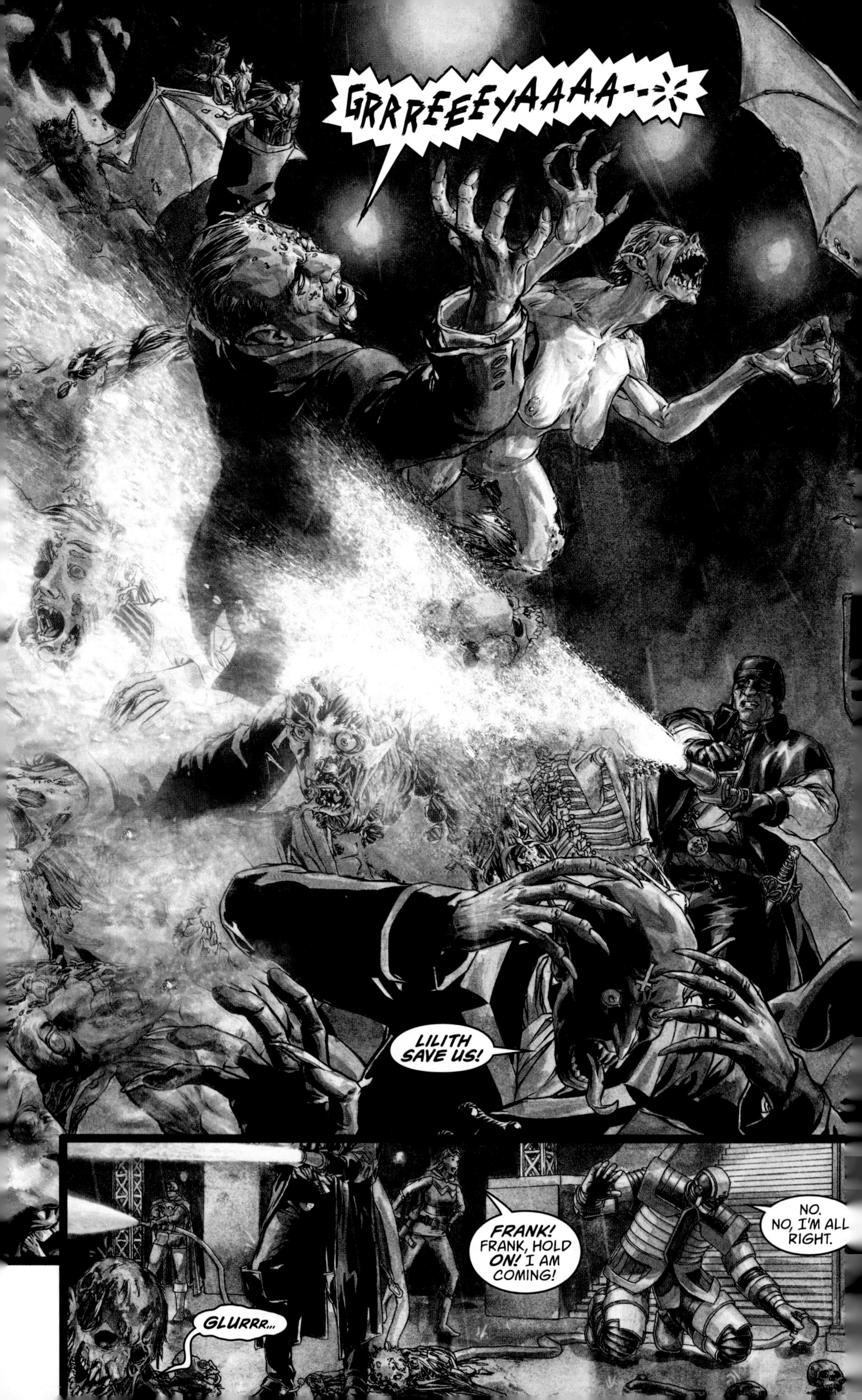
GRRREEEYAAAA--
LILITH SAVE US!
FRANK! FRANK, HOLD ON! I AM COMING!
NO. NO, I'M ALL RIGHT.
GLURRR...

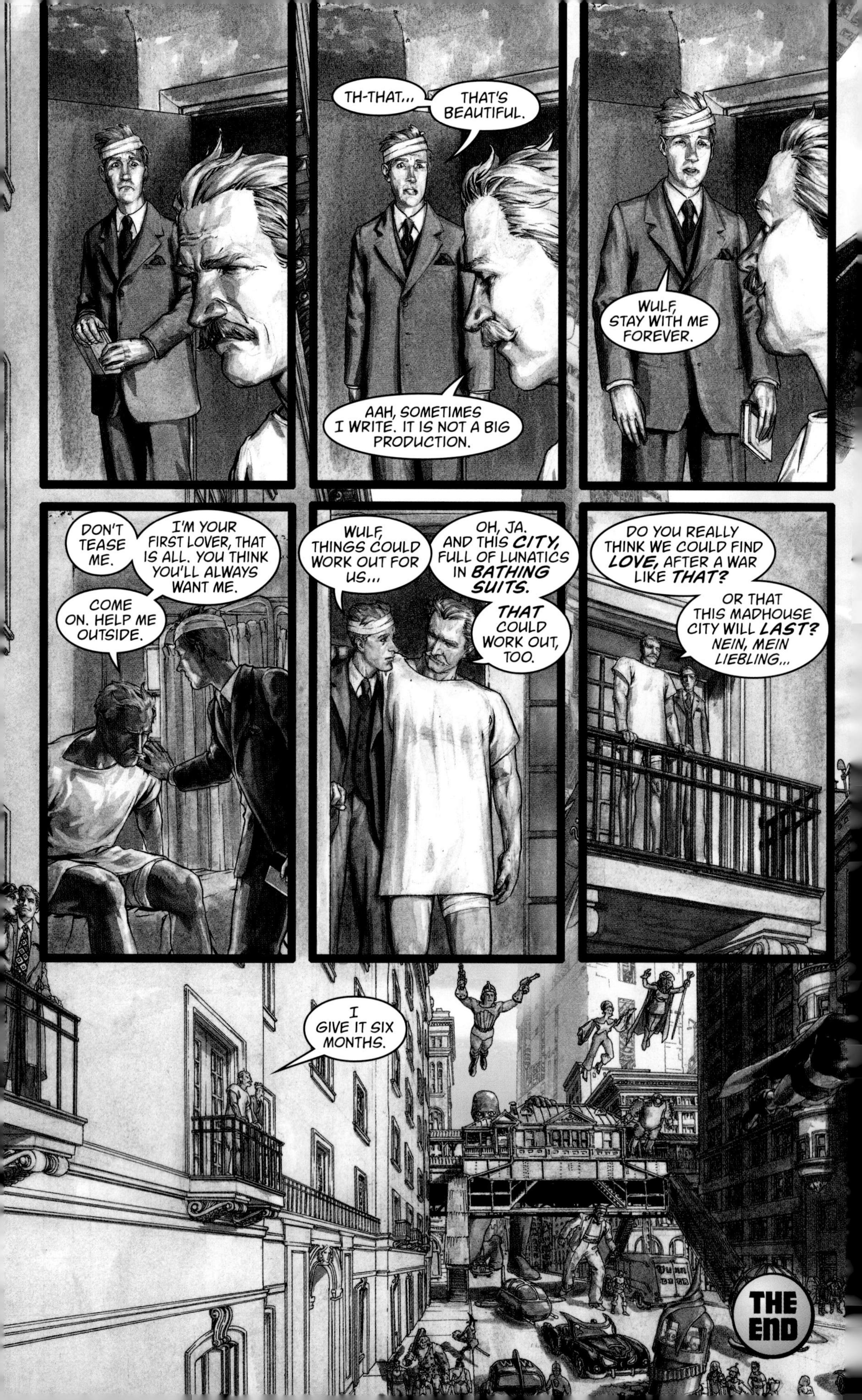
TH-THAT...
THAT'S BEAUTIFUL.
AAH, SOMETIMES I WRITE. IT IS NOT A BIG PRODUCTION.
WULF, STAY WITH ME FOREVER.
DON'T TEASE ME.
I'M YOUR FIRST LOVER, THAT IS ALL. YOU THINK YOU'LL ALWAYS WANT ME.
COME ON. HELP ME OUTSIDE.
WULF, THINGS COULD WORK OUT FOR US...
OH, JA. AND THIS CITY, FULL OF LUNATICS IN BATHING SUITS.
THAT COULD WORK OUT, TOO.
DO YOU REALLY THINK WE COULD FIND LOVE, AFTER A WAR LIKE THAT?
OR THAT THIS MADHOUSE CITY WILL LAST? NEIN, MEIN LIEBLING...
I GIVE IT SIX MONTHS.
THE END

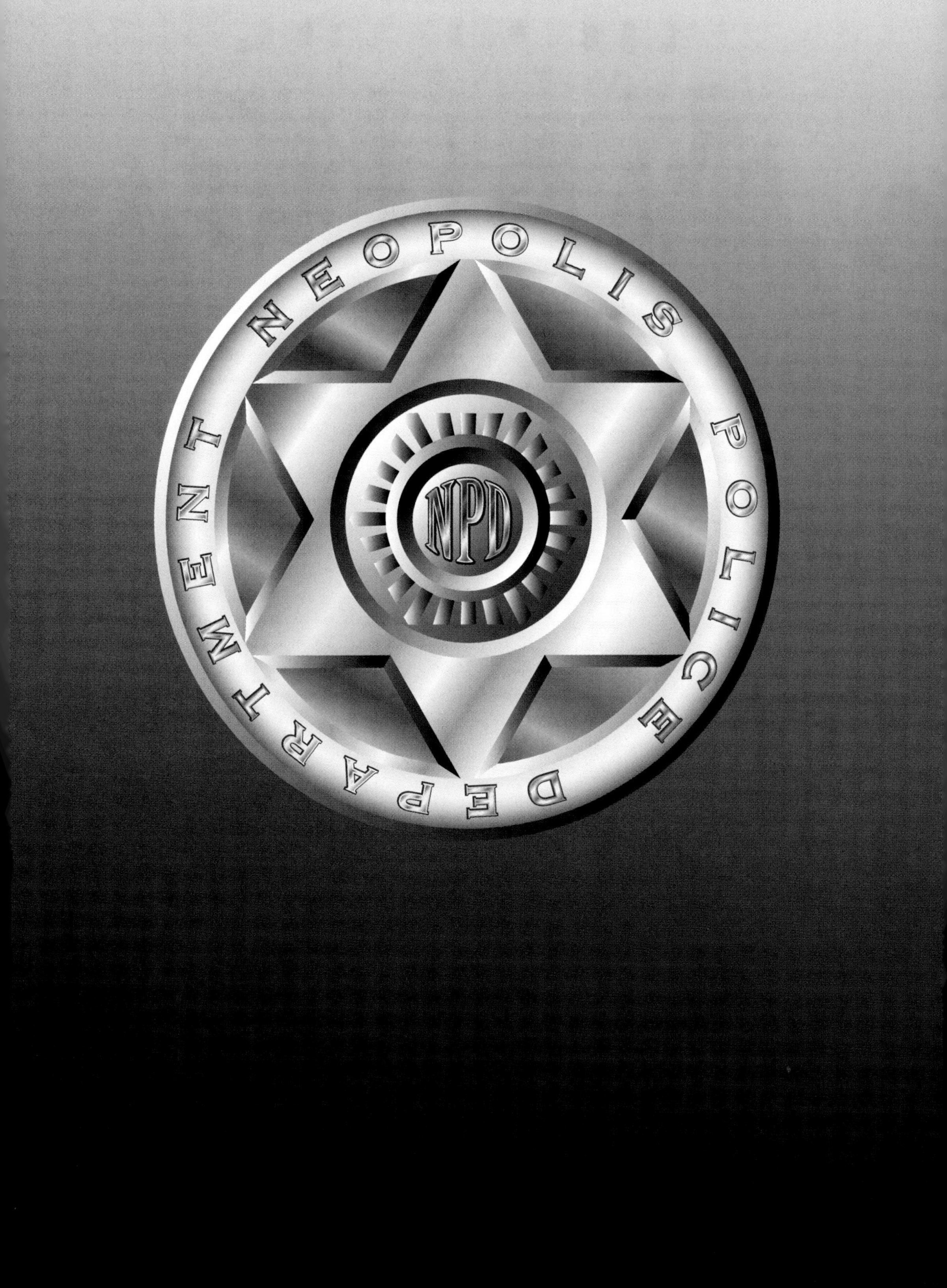
NEOPOLIS POLICE DEPARTMENT
NPD

CONTRIBUTORS

ALAN MOORE is perhaps the most acclaimed writer in the graphic story medium, having garnered many awards for works such as WATCHMEN, V FOR VENDETTA, FROM HELL, MIRACLEMAN, SWAMP THING and SUPREME. He is currently masterminding the America's Best Comics line, with writing credits that include PROMETHEA, TOM STRONG, TOP 10, THE LEAGUE OF EXTRAORDINARY GENTLEMEN and TOMORROW STORIES. Alan is also overseeing and plotting the upcoming series ALBION, written by Leah Moore and John Reppion. He lives in central England.

GENE HA is the Eisner Award-winning artist and co-creator of TOP 10 and THE FORTY-NINERS. Recently he has also drawn GLOBAL FREQUENCY and covers for Wizard Magazine and Marvel Comics. Gene feels very odd talking about himself in the third person. He draws at a small table in Oak Park, Illinois, and rants about comics and politics at www.geneha.com. His patient and lovely wife Lisa and their two beagle-bassets take care of Gene as he gets older and crankier.

ART LYON, colorist of THE FORTY-NINERS, has been in and out of the comic book industry for twenty years as a penciler, inker, colorist, retailer, and all-around sequential guy. He recently returned to comics as a colorist with GLOBAL FREQUENCY #12, and a pin-up in the ASTRO CITY GUIDEBOOK. Ellen Starr Lyon, a talented painter in her own right, has been his assistant on GLOBAL FREQUENCY and THE FORTY-NINERS, handling the lion's share of the ink washes. They married in 1999, live in Bloomington, Indiana, and have two delightful children, Finnian and Odessa.

TODD KLEIN has lettered and designed nearly all of the ABC line of comics and collected editions. He began lettering comics in 1977 and has won numerous Eisner, Harvey and CBG Fan awards for his work. Todd lives in rural southern New Jersey with his wife Ellen and a small menagerie of animals.

Now that you've read about the early days of the Neopolis Police Department, don't miss their action-packed present-day exploits in these ABC Editions!

Members of today's Top 10 Police Force also appear in these ABC Editions!

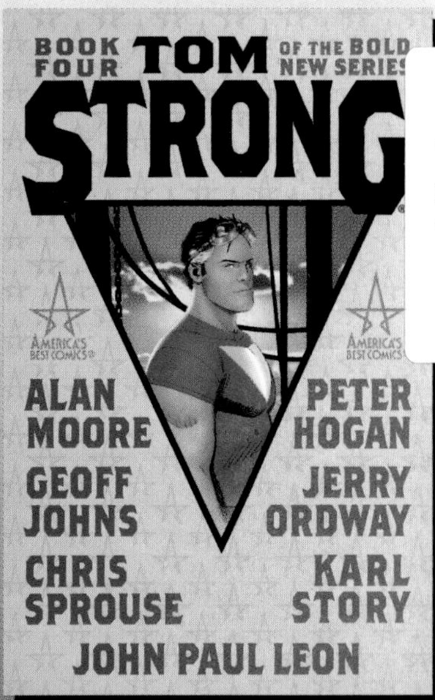
BOOK FOUR
TOM STRONG
OF THE BOLD NEW SERIES
AMERICA'S BEST COMICS
ALAN MOORE
PETER HOGAN
GEOFF JOHNS
JERRY ORDWAY
CHRIS SPROUSE
KARL STORY
JOHN PAUL LEON

TOM STRONG
BOOKS 1 to 4
Moore/Sprouse/Gordon/
Story/Various

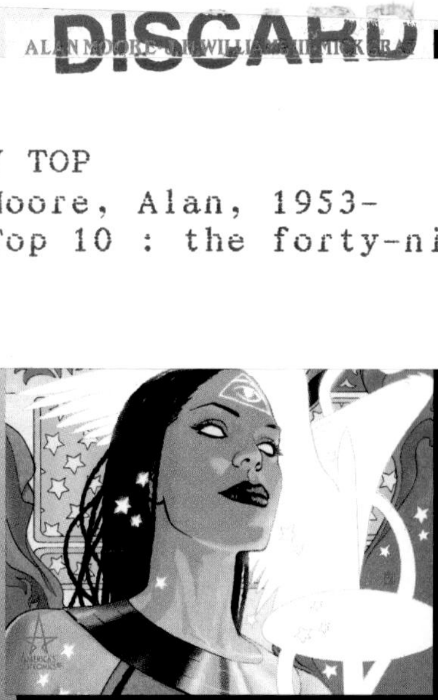

PROMETHEA
BOOKS 1 to 4
Moore/Williams III/Gray
Cox/Villarrubia

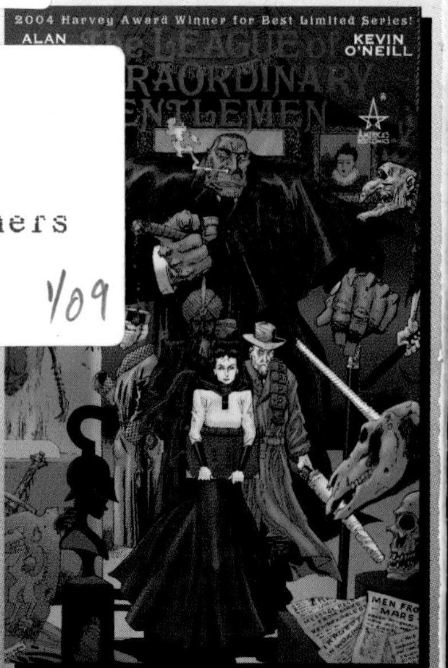
2004 Harvey Award Winner for Best Limited Series!
ALAN
KEVIN O'NEILL
MEN FROM MARS

THE LEAGUE OF
EXTRAORDINARY GENTLEMEN
VOLUMES 1 & 2
Moore/O'Neill

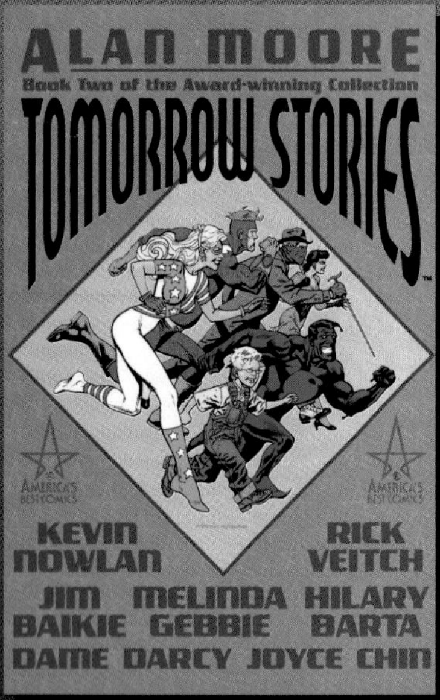
ALAN MOORE
Book Two of the Award-winning Collection
TOMORROW STORIES
KEVIN NOWLAN
RICK VEITCH
JIM BAIKIE
MELINDA GEBBIE
HILARY BARTA
DAME DARCY
JOYCE CHIN

TOMORROW STORIES
BOOKS 1 & 2
Moore/Various

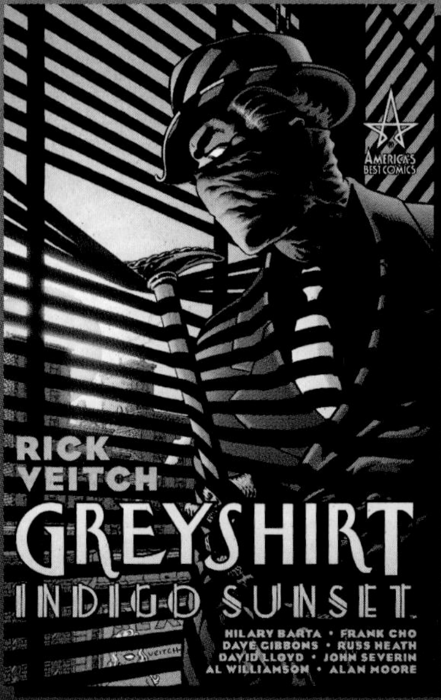
AMERICA'S BEST COMICS
RICK VEITCH
GREYSHIRT
INDIGO SUNSET
HILARY BARTA • FRANK CHO
DAVE GIBBONS • RUSS HEATH
DAVID LLOYD • JOHN SEVERIN
AL WILLIAMSON • ALAN MOORE

GREYSHIRT:
INDIGO SUNSET
Veitch/Various

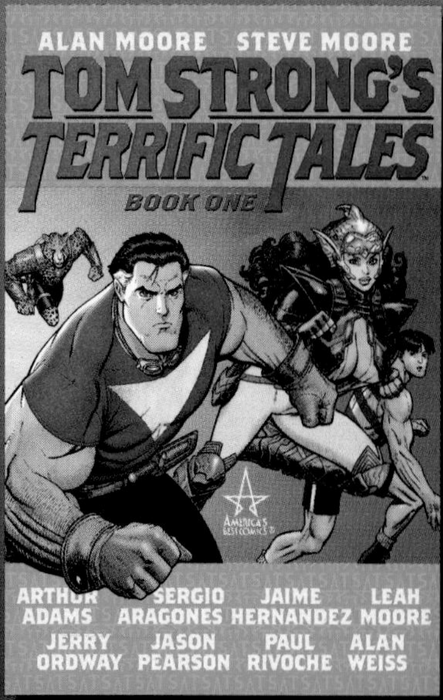
ALAN MOORE
STEVE MOORE
TOM STRONG'S TERRIFIC TALES
BOOK ONE
ARTHUR ADAMS
SERGIO ARAGONES
JAIME HERNANDEZ
LEAH MOORE
JERRY ORDWAY
JASON PEARSON
PAUL RIVOCHE
ALAN WEISS

TOM STRONG'S TERRIFIC
TALES BOOKS 1 & 2
Moore/Moore/Various

To find more books and comics from
America's Best Comics, call 1-888-COMIC BOOK
for the comics retailer nearest to you
or visit your local book store.

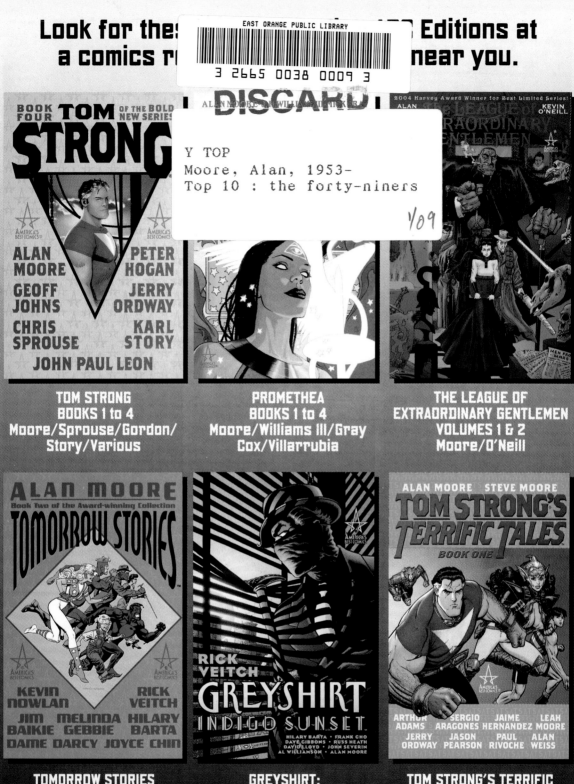